UNIQUE

6 Simple Steps
to Creating a Highly Effective Personal Brand

MELANIE GOEL

Text © Melanie Goel, 2020

Illustration © Neda Hajmomeni, 2020

The moral rights of the author have been asserted.

All rights reserved. No part of this book may be reproduced by any mechanical, photographic or electronic process, or in the form of phonographic recording; public or private use, other than for 'fair use' as brief quotations embodied in articles, reviews, without prior written permission of the author.

The information given in this book should not be treated as substitute for professional medical advice; always consult a medical practitioner. Any use of information in this book is at the reader's discretion and risk. The author cannot be held responsible for any loss, claim or damage arising out of the use, or misuse, of the suggestions made, the failure to take medical advice or for any material on third-party websites.

ISBN: 9798697684801

About the Author

Melanie is a seasoned Personal Branding Strategist and ex-Tesla marketer. Having worked for one of the most powerful personal brands, Elon Musk, she started coaching individuals on how to build a highly effective personal brand and promote their skills and full potential. With her coaching programs she has helped founders, side hustlers, influencers and aspiring individuals around the world to more success and effective careers.

Melanie lives in Munich, Germany with her husband and dog.

CONTENTS

Contents	I
Introduction	1

SECTION 1 – Theory and Basics About Building Highly Effective Personal Brands

All You Need to Know About Personal Branding	6
What It Takes to Build a Highly Effective Personal Brand	11
What Makes a Brand Highly Effective	16
What Makes a Brand Highly Ineffective	18

SECTION 2 – The Magic of a Personal Value Proposition

6 Simple Steps to Your Highly Effective Personal Brand	26
Step 1: Setting Goals for a Powerful Value Proposition	28
Step 2: Defining Values	35
Step 3: Shaping Your Image	52
Step 4: Matching Your Skills	63
Step 5: Exploring Your Added Value	75
Step 6: Discovering Your Market Fit	79
Conclusion	85

SECTION 3 – Use Your Highly Effective Personal Brand

5 Situations Where Personal Branding Makes You More Successful	90
Tips and Tricks to Staying Consistent	99

SECTION 4 – Conclusion and Appendix

Referenced & Suggested Reading List	105

Introduction

Why write a book about the power of personal branding?

Before I answer these questions, let me tell you a little story first. This is a story that made me quit my stable, well-paid job to become a personal branding coach, and write this book.

I've worked in marketing, branding and communications my entire career. I worked at agencies, startups and big companies like Tesla. Although my experience spans different industries and different companies, there was one recurring theme among my coworkers: there was always a group of people who were motivated and extremely talented but unable to promote themselves properly due to shyness. As I watched the progression of their careers, I saw less qualified people overtaking them. And, because I love observing people, I started to notice that this phenomenon wasn't just limited to workplaces. I noticed it with friends who tried to make it on social media or tried to promote side projects. I noticed it with entrepreneurs who tried to convince investors or incredibly educated people who failed to get a job simply because they didn't have the means and knowledge to highlight their best competencies when it mattered.

I observed this scenario for a while and was really upset by it. I truly believe that everyone deserves a fair chance and what I was seeing wasn't fair. Why should the loudest people always win? Why should more qualified individuals suffer only because they happen to be introverted or simply more modest? You don't have to be a show-off to be successful, you just need to learn how to promote your best self to the right people at the right time in the right way.

> *I wrote this book to give you and everyone else out there a fair shot at succeeding against the loud ones*

But before we get started, I'd like to explain what you'll get in this book. It's important to understand that personal branding is not something that will give you instant gratification. The path to personal branding involves a strategic and logical step by step process, which I have broken down for you in this simple guide. I promise that with a little patience, this process works. Let's take a quick look at why.

Attention spans are short – I think we can all agree on that. So if you want to be heard, your first job is to overcome this challenge. In the beginning, when you are just starting out with your personal brand, you need to do everything to get attention. You have to be compelling, easy to grasp, and catchy in order to be seen as worthy of other people's precious attention. That's where your personal brand messaging and value proposition come into play (I'll explain what this is later). But once you've convinced your audience, and they start trusting that you're worthy of their attention, you've managed to get a spot in their brain. Now, they will start recognizing you. Getting recognized amongst the loud ones is one of the main achievements of personal branding. Only when people recognize you, will they be receptive to these messages. And once they begin to trust you, they'll gradually trust those messages as well. People will actually start listening to what you have to say.

You can compare this concept to social media marketing. Most companies want to launch lead generation campaigns right away because they want to see immediate results, right? But really, how often have you purchased something from a company you've never heard of before? Brand awareness must be prioritized! The same thing happens in public relations. Some companies just keep sending out press releases and they wonder why no one's writing about them. No one is writing about them because the respective company never made an effort to introduce itself and raise awareness about what it does. What happened in the cases of social media marketing and public relations is that these companies skipped a crucial step: the step of creating awareness first. People need to know you're trustworthy and qualified before they start interacting with or even noticing you. And that's what we want in the end, right?

If we want to convince people, we need to go that extra mile and first gain their trust. An authentic brand and consistent messaging does that for you. It's a long-term investment, but it pays off big time. With a personal brand you can be the Apple and the Coca-Cola in the world of individuals. You can be the person who is spotted immediately in a crowd. With a personal brand, you don't have to beg for attention anymore because once it's established, your brand's identity does that for you. With a personal brand, your voice will be heard and remembered.

That being said, let me explain what you can expect from this book and where you'll be able to find it. In the first chapter, I present everything you need to know about personal branding and what makes it highly effective in a theoretical manner (I'll make it exciting, I promise). In the second chapter, I walk you through the process of building a highly effective personal brand. This is complemented by a lot of actionable advice and helpful exercises. Finally, in the third chapter, I share tips and tricks on how to make your personal brand an integral part of your daily life.

Let's get started!

SECTION 1

Theory and Basics About Building Highly Effective Personal Brands

All You Need to Know About Personal Branding

First, let's start with the hard truth: A brand is intangible. A brand is not measurable or quantifiable like ad clicks or bounce rates. A brand is not a 'thing' that can be touched, held or heard.

I mention this right at the beginning because it's the question I get asked the most. Remember the example from above? A personal brand is a long-term investment that creates awareness and trust, but it's not something that will show up on your Google Analytics dashboard right from the start.

I understand that the lack of quantifiability might be off-putting for you. After all, most of us are used to measuring success in numbers. But the truth is:

A brand might not be tangible, but you're nothing without one.

A brand is your identity. It is the perception and the experience people associate with you, your company or product. The feeling people get from interacting with a brand is the reason some people fly Lufthansa, for example, even though much cheaper alternatives exist. It is also the reason why certain people get promoted at work even though there are more skilled and eligible candidates to choose from. Simply said: as the positive experiences with your brand accumulate, you will have more success over time.

A Brand Determines Your Level of Success

A brand's image represents a long-term strategy, or as Elon Musk said: "A brand is just a perception, and perception will match reality over time".

In short, a brand signifies how an individual or a business is perceived by those who experience it. A brand makes you identifiable and differentiates you from the crowd. You can shape that perception by continuously feeding it with consistent brand messaging. The result: the experience and the values associated with that experience will gradually be perceived as real.

What exactly does that mean? Let's say you want to brand yourself as a diligent tech blogger. To convince people that you are just that, you post new, relevant articles every week over the course of a year, with no breaks in between. Eventually, your followers will perceive you as diligent and as a tech writer. By being consistent, your audience will see you as a real tech blogger.

Your brand is your most valuable asset

The leading US business thinker and writer Tom Peters once said: "All of us need to understand the importance of branding. We are CEOs of our own companies: Me Inc. To be in business today, our most important job is to be [the] head marketer for the brand called You."

Best-selling author of 4-hour Work Week, Tim Ferriss, goes even further by stating: "Personal branding is about managing your name - even if you don't own a business - in a world of misinformation, disinformation, and semi-permanent Google records. Going on a date? Chances are that your 'blind' date has googled your name. Going to a job interview? Ditto."

To understand the truth of these statements, let's briefly dive into psychology.

Plant Your Brand in Your Audience's Mind

In our communication-saturated society, there's nothing more crucial than communication. Sounds contradictory? Sure, but I'm not talking about communication that just adds on to the noise that already exists. I'm talking about the opposite kind.

What has become rare is clear, concise and concrete communication. Communication that is to the point and easy for the receiver to grasp. Why has it become rare? It's difficult to achieve! In order to communicate and position a message in a clear manner, we have to dig deep and understand the target group, our values, our motivations, our goals and most importantly the reason why we want to communicate.

It's much easier to remain on the surface and create content, just for the sake of creating content. But that's not how you plant your brand in your audience's mind.

Yes, numerous studies reveal that the more often you appear and the more often your audience gets to interact with you, the more likely it is that they will. But if your communication isn't effective and your messaging isn't easy to grasp, that strategy won't get you anywhere.

That's why it's important to take the time to map out your brand and your brand messaging and then go nuts with the content!

Be the Convenient Choice

Let's take a look at how branding can help you stand out from that content noise - your message has to be easy to grasp and sticky! Only then will you see engagement with your brand.

In the famous book 'Positioning', Al Ries and Jack Trout explain that in order to make a message stick, you need to find a hook in your audience's mind.

An over communicated mind is ruled by short attention spans. When it comes to personal branding, you can use that to your advantage.

How? Your message needs to be so easy to understand and grasp that the receiver immediately understands what you're trying to convey. Your ideal scenario is that the receiver understands you and your message without thinking any further and without any effort on their part.

Whatever your message is, it must be clear, short, relevant and positive.

Let's take a networking scenario. There's one person in the room who's particularly sought after. Let's say because they're an investor, a manager who's in charge of promotion, a scout, a designer, whatever it may be. For you, this means competition because you'll compete for an opportunity to speak with them. You'll compete for their attention span. You'll compete for a chance to be remembered. One way to do that is by introducing yourself with a brand message that is so relevant and short that they can decide in a split second whether you're worth talking to. Luckily for you, many of your competitors will not be able to introduce themselves like that! And that's where you become the more convenient choice!

By making an effort to create a concise brand message, you reduce the effort others need to make to understand why you're interesting.

If you can minimize your audience's efforts and provide them with a positive experience that is associated with your personal brand, they will associate positive images with your brand and eventually perceive you as the better and convenient option.

And the easier you make it for someone, the more successful you'll be. Because who likes to make things more difficult anyway?

Create New Realities

So far we've learned that a brand is a perception, that perceptions are made, stored and shaped in our minds and that the more we interact with a brand, the more authentic we perceive its image to be. Based on this fact, we can say that branding has the power to shape reality.

But be careful here, it's important to keep in mind that the perception is created by the audience, not by you. You can influence the perception through brand messaging, your brand identity and your actions, but, in the end, the audience decides how they perceive you. Interestingly enough, that can be positive or negative!

Conclusion

That's why it is important to think branding through as a first step. It is essential that you define the messaging carefully and align all of your actions with it. The more consistently your audience experiences and interacts with your brand, the more their perception will resemble the image you want them to have.

Let's look at the diligent tech blogger example from before. Let's say his audience receives a newsletter with worthwhile content every single Monday. No matter what happens in his personal life, the email goes out. Due to his steadfast commitment, his readers eventually perceive him as a diligent writer and consider his blog a reliable source.

Or, let's say you're an aspiring fashion blogger for secondhand and fair fashion and you showcase the clothing you promote in every single social media post. Eventually, your audience will perceive you as an influencer for sustainable clothing.

Your brand, your brand identity, your messaging, if implemented strategically and thoughtfully, and if lived by consistently, will create a unique experience that will be planted in people's heads. If the experience is positive, customers will come back to you, no matter what other options they're presented with.

You'll be able to tie people to your brand and encourage them to talk about your brand and spread the word. With time, a powerful and authentic brand image will help you become more successful.

What It Takes to Build a Highly Effective Personal Brand

Okay, now we know what a brand is, but what does a brand consist of? What are the essential elements of a brand?

In this chapter, we'll look at the most important aspects of a powerful personal brand and the role they play in branding.

Before you can deliver a positive brand experience, you must first understand what makes a brand experience positive. I already pointed out how intangible branding is and that it often comes across as a vague concept. It doesn't have to be this way. A brand consists of nothing more than a clear and simple set of concepts.

In this section, I show you what these tools, or essential elements, are and how you can apply this insight to your brand.

The most essential elements for a powerful personal brand must be comprehensively unique and include:

1. Value proposition and positioning
2. Brand identity, brand voice and brand message
3. Brand promise and brand purpose
4. Name, tagline, logo and visual appearance

Each of these elements are important aspects of successful personal branding. In this chapter, I introduce you to the general concepts. In chapter two, we'll get more hands-on, and I'll show you how to incorporate these elements into your brand through exercises and examples.

Value Proposition

The value proposition is the most important aspect of a brand. It provides the foundation for how you position your brand. It is the impression you want others to have. It truly is the backbone of every brand.

A value proposition states in a few sentences (ideally 2-3 short ones) who you are, what you stand for, which problems you solve and how others can benefit from that.

Authenticity is key here. That means that a value proposition must align with your individual values. Once you build a personal brand, you must live and promote a consistent brand image at all times. If a brand's image is based on disingenuous values, you'll eventually make mistakes and your brand experience will feel inconsistent. Your audience will get upset, or may even feel betrayed. Worst case, your brand's reputation will be ruined entirely.

You will notice that I will repeat this point throughout the book, but there's absolutely nothing more important for a personal brand than authenticity. Always keep that in mind over the course of creating your own brand.

Brand Identity, Brand Voice, Brand Message and Brand Image

Brand identity, voice and message are closely linked to your value proposition. The value proposition is basically the foundation on which those three branding elements are built.

The main function of a brand identity, voice and message is that you become identifiable. Whenever someone interacts with your brand, regardless through which means, they should be able to recognize you instantly. A brand's image is the vibe you and your entire brand project. It is the experience your audience notices and judges.

But now let's get a bit more specific.

The **brand identity** is essentially the embodiment of your value proposition. Once you've defined which values your brand should be associated with, you start creating a persona or identity that fits with this value set. In a personal brand, that's easy because the persona is based on yourself. However, to create a consistent identity you have to ask: if I want to uphold this brand, how should I interact with people? How should I react to different scenarios?

Let's say you are building a brand as a tech blogger. In this case, you'd ask yourself what type of identity should that tech blogger embody. To be more specific, you'd define what kind of writer you'd be.

Defining your **brand voice and messaging** is the next step. Once you get clarity on your brand identity, you need to decide how a person with that identity and value set would communicate. Did you choose an analytical, straightforward tech blogger identity? Then brainstorm what kind of words someone like that would use? How long would this person's posts be? What kind of imagery would he use? Which colours are appropriate? Would a tech blogger with that brand image use a reserved, professional or rather a colloquial, easy-going tone and writing style?

Remember to choose something that is authentic to you because in a personal brand, the identity, voice and message resembles you. If you fake it, you'll break it.

A **brand image** is when all of the elements above come together in a cohesive way. The brand image is the experience your audience has with you. It's their perception of how they were treated when interacting with your brand and their judgement of how pleasant or unpleasant it was to engage with it.

That being said: Make this count! Be authentic, consistent and positive!

Brand Promise and Brand Purpose

These two are often confused, but they serve very different purposes for your brand.

A **brand purpose** is the WHY of your brand. Why are you doing what you're doing? What do you stand for beyond making money? What is your motivation? What are your drivers in life?

The answers to those questions are your brand purpose. They make you approachable, relatable and human. And an authentic and relatable brand purpose makes it easy for people to associate themselves with your brand on an emotional level and to identify with your personality and values.

The brand purpose is really where your personal identity, mindset and values shine through and make a difference in how others perceive you.

A **brand promise** on the other hand is more about the expectations people have of you and your brand. It is about what you promise your brand will deliver.

Let's say you promise to deliver high-quality tech reviews every Monday. This is what people expect from you. They expect you to be diligent and skilled enough to write high-quality articles.

A promise makes your brand tangible, but also more controllable because you can influence your audience's expectations. For example, you can achieve this through setting expectations in FAQs, a value statement, a 'What to expect" page and so on.

To summarize: The brand purpose is the emotional connection with your brand and the brand promise is a tool used to set expectations.

Name, Tagline and Visual Appearance

Even though a name, tagline and logo are a vital part of a brand's identity and image, I decided to describe them last because, in most cases, they're not as relevant for **personal brands**.

In personal branding, you don't really need to look for a **brand name** since you yourself are the brand. The need to find a brand name only applies if you decide to adopt an artist name. However, if you're working on a side project or if you want to give your blog or project a name that is different from yours, be sure to remember your values before choosing a name. I will elaborate more on values later in the book.

Let's refer again to the tech blogger example. If you want to create an analytical, straight-forward image with a reserved and analytical tone, it would be inconsistent to choose a name like 'Freaky Tech Blizzard' (*fictional) as the name for your blog. You might want to go with something more down-to-earth in this case.

A **tagline** however is important, especially for your social media profiles.

In personal branding, you derive your tagline from your value proposition (which we'll work on throughout the course of this book). Your tagline can either be the first sentence of your value statement or an additional, even more concise version specifically created for social media.

In the last step, you should think about the **visual appearance** of your brand. You need to decide where you want to appear and how.

Which platforms do you want to be present on? What are the best practices there? Are there certain standards of appearance that you need to adhere to? Is imagery required for those platforms? If so, how will you get it and what does it have to look like in order to align with your brand image?

Then you need to think about questions like, do you want to have a logo? If so, how can it portray your values and the main message of your value proposition? If your platform is Instagram, which filters most resonate with your brand image? Which ones give the most consistent experience with your brand values?

Conclusion

The most important tool for your personal brand is your value proposition. All of the other branding elements are encompassed by this in one way or another. To create a powerful value proposition, all the other elements need to be rock solid.

However, the value proposition is also the most difficult part of creating a brand. It requires you to be honest and real with yourself so that your audience will experience an honest, real, and authentic brand in the end.

But good news for you: I've developed a framework and step by step system that is solely designed to get you to that powerful value proposition. It provides you with easy guidelines to nailing this hard task.

Let's get to it!

What Makes a Brand Highly Effective

Okay, so we've covered some basics about branding and branding essentials. But what makes a brand highly effective? Why are some brands successful and others not?

It sounds simple but what I'm going to tell you next is the essence of what makes or breaks a brand: clarity, authenticity and consistency.

Let's take a look at what that means and why it's so hard to achieve.

Brand Clarity

First and foremost, you must have clarity. Specifically, you must have clarity on the goal of your brand. Why do you want a brand and what should the brand help you achieve?

Next, you need clarity on what you want your brand to stand for. What do you want people to associate with your brand? Which values are essential for the brand you want to promote?

You also need clarity on your brand image, voice and messaging. As we've discussed in the previous chapter, your message needs to be concise, short and easy to grasp. It should be so clear that your audience doesn't need to make any effort to understand why you're awesome and helpful to them.

Clarity is hard work. It requires serious commitment and time to dig below the surface but let me tell you, you'll be rewarded with a powerful brand that really stands out simply because very few people go this extra mile!

Brand Authenticity

Everything rises and falls with the authenticity of your brand. With a personal brand, you are promoting yourself. Whatever brand image, messaging and value statement you choose, you will need to live up to it. You'll need to promote that image every time and everywhere.

No matter which industry you choose to work in, products and services live off of emotions and some humanness. People want to buy from people and know who they're buying from. If the values you chose or the images you've created are fake, you're prone to make mistakes. You're prone to be inconsistent. And that can seriously damage your brand and its overall success.

It takes effort and dedication to create a brand but it only takes a split second to ruin it. Be aware of this! If you don't want to waste your time, be honest with yourself right from the start.

Who are you and who are you not? If you're serious about building a brand, always base your values on who you are. Don't copy others or build a brand image of something you wish you were. You are unique in your own way, utilize that and it will pay off.

Brand Consistency

Lastly, once you're done defining your brand, be consistent! Be consistent with your messaging, be consistent in your outreach, get inside of the customer's mind and stay there. Occupy that room we've talked about. Create lots and lots of positive interactions with your brand.

This is hard simply because you have a life outside of work. And that life doesn't care about your intentions to be consistent. Things will be thrown in your way, obstacles, hurdles, life events. These unexpected inconveniences will make you want to prioritise other things; they might make you question the purpose of building your own brand.

Stay consistent! Great brands aren't built overnight. They are built on consistency. Try to create habits and environments that make it easy to stick to your routines, tasks and activities.

Like bestselling author James Clear explained in 'Atomic Habits': "Every action requires a certain amount of energy! The more energy required, the less likely it is to occur. […] In the beginning, when you're motivated and excited, you can muster the strength to get started. But after a few days, such a massive effort feels exhausting. [...] The less energy a habit requires, the more likely it is to occur."

Try to create that environment and then STAY CONSISTENT.

What Makes a Brand Highly Ineffective

There are reasons why brands fail and there are reasons why brands succeed.

Successful brands influence the lives, minds and behaviour of their audience. In the previous chapter, we discussed what makes brands highly effective. Now, we'll take a look at what makes them highly ineffective.

Over the course of my career, I've observed two very common mistakes that reversed a brand's success. These are inauthentic value choices and copying other brands.

Inauthentic Value Choice

What does it mean to select inauthentic values?

Later in the book we'll dive deep into the role of values for a brand, but what I can already say here is: Authenticity is key! The values you choose for your brand must align with your own personal values. The actions that come from living your values must come naturally to you. This makes it easy for you to incorporate your branding into everything you do because you don't have to think twice. This allows for a consistent brand image.

This sounds reasonable, right? And still so few people care about this when creating their brand. Let's take a look at what usually happens. When we consume media, we analyse what the market is currently looking for and what line of thinking, type of pictures and style of writing is gaining momentum. As a result, we try to position ourselves and our brand with a messaging that fits exactly that.

Don't get me wrong, it is incredibly important to look at the market's current standards. BUT there's a reason that 'finding a market fit' is the last step of this uniqueness framework.

There might have been a few lucky ones who succeeded with this approach but it is a risky and short-term oriented move. A brand is a long-term investment. The messaging you choose for your brand needs to represent your brand's values consistently for a long time. If you choose whatever's trending, there will never be consistency - neither in your messaging, nor in your actions. And the latter is what really counts and makes people stick with you over other alternatives.

Imagine if Coca Cola changed its messaging and packaging with every new trend. Would you be able to recognise the brand? Probably not. Because the colours, the tone and the bottle's unique shape is exactly how we recognise Coca Cola.

Or, do you think that a personal brand like Barack Obama's would have worked so well if he had changed his stance and his way of communicating every other month? Definitely not. We recognise him for being calm, intelligent and witty because this is the persona he portrays every single time, across every medium and in every situation he's presented with, irrespective of what's going on in the world or his life.

For a personal and a business brand, it's crucial to first look inwards before looking outwards. You first have to build the foundation of what your brand is supposed to embody. A personal brand must first be authentic to you, and have a market fit second.

We'll discuss how to do that in greater detail later.

Brand Copying

Closely linked to inauthentic value choices is the common mistake of simply copying other people and personal brands.

If you've read the section above, you might already have an idea of why these strategies do not work over a longer stretch of time.

Good brands looked inwards before they looked outwards. The people behind successful brands took the time to define their values. They also took the time to align all of their messaging with what they stand for and what their opportunity sweet spots will respond to.

If you copy another brand when creating your own, you'll communicate your brand in a sweet spot that's already taken and occupied by an authentic brand. I call such a brand authentic because it fits **their** brand's actions, messaging and image. In contrast, you look like a phony. So, it's not surprising that you will be less successful, is it?

It's fine to have similarities with other brands. It's also inevitable that your brand will have something in common with other brands if you're in the same industry or are maybe even competing for the same job, audience etc., but what makes you different is you. Your personal twist on a brand that exists already is your personal value set, your individual skills and your unique personality. That's why it's so important to look inwards.

Look inward, then outward and occupy your own opportunity sweet spot while letting others do their thing!

SECTION 2

Create Your Highly Effective Personal Brand

The Magic of a Personal Value Proposition

In the previous chapters, we discussed that a value proposition is the foundation of a brand. As the name says, a value proposition is based on values. And not just any values – **your** values.

If you want to build an authentic brand, you need to fully support those values and stand behind them. You need to embody and live them in such a way that people describe you in the words of your values. You need to be so convincing that people believe that you **are** those values.

Whenever that happens, you know that you did a good job branding yourself.

That being said, it's not too surprising that the most important 'tool' for a brand is called a value proposition (isn't it funny that the word is right there in our faces and still so few people take the time to define clear values for their brands?).

A value proposition is basically your unique selling point and vision combined in a short statement. It should be short enough to introduce your brand without exhausting anyone's attention span.

But apart from it being short, a value proposition needs to be memorable, catchy and simple. There's no room for complicated or overly sophisticated words.

The ultimate goal of a value proposition is that after a prospective customer learns about your brand, they remember who you are, what you stand for and what you can do for them.

Let's visualize this for a moment.

Imagine you're again at that networking event from earlier and this time a well-known personality in that circle comes up to **you**. Maybe you're already getting a bit nervous because they show an interest in talking to you. They stop in front of you, shake your hand and ask: "What do you do?"

How would you answer?

If I think back to the times before I started my personal branding journey, my most common answer was: 'Umm..soo...yeah...soo..how should I best say that..umm..'. And with that, the attention and interest of my conversation partner was gone and the chance to build a meaningful conversation with it.

Most of the time we only have one chance. And that chance lasts a split-second. In that split-second people judge you. They judge who you are, if you're capable or not, if you're smart or not, even if you're likeable or not and worth talking to.

If I'm honest, I do it too. We all do it.

And to make this split-second count, we need a value proposition.

How Will You Benefit From a Value Proposition?

There are various benefits to having a value proposition.

First, you stand out. How? Remember the networking example from before? 99% of people will introduce themselves similar to how I used to. If you have a value proposition and you can repeat it directly upon being asked what you do, your conversation partner will be very impressed. They'll remember you as the one person, the 1%, who knows what they want and stand for.

Second, you make it easy for people to connect with you. Let's consider the networking example again and let's assume that you've introduced yourself stammeringly and without a clear message. In that case, there are two likely reactions from the other person. Either they stop listening and think about other things, or they listen, but end up with multiple, unrelated snippets of information about you. What they would have to do next is either ask you questions to fill in the holes of the story or try to make sense of it by themselves. Sounds like a lot of effort!

What do you think the most common reaction is? What do you do when someone introduces themselves vaguely and paints a confused picture? If your answer is 'stop listening and think about other things', you're part of the majority.

With a value proposition, you solve this problem and eliminate the need for your conversation partner to make any unnecessary effort. A value proposition ensures that your conversation partner knows everything they need to know to make an immediate initial judgement. Obviously, there's much more to you than just this statement, but this is how you get your foot in the door. If you deliver your value proposition correctly, opportunities will open up. People will be hooked and interested in learning more about you.

Third, you will look more professional. What does a professional person look like to you? If you had to describe them, what traits do they have?

One 'professional' trait is to be able to articulate yourself. If you know when to say what in an appropriate manner, people tend to listen to you more intently. Another trait is being able to listen. People like to talk, especially about themselves. If you make your introduction concise, short and easy to understand, you give others more time to talk about who **they** are.

Fourth, you will build long-lasting relationships. If you make it easy for people to understand who you are and what you bring to the table, and if you're able to deliver that in a professional manner, they will take you seriously and will be interested in keeping in touch. Once people understand that your initial introduction (value proposition) was actually authentic and that you have the skills you claimed to have, you'll most likely be looking at a new long-term acquaintance (or whatever you want that person to be).

Why is that so? If you think about the people you meet day in and out, how many of them are authentic? How many deliver on what they say they'll do? How many of them are honest? Not many, right?

Running the risk of repeating myself indefinitely, I am here to remind you that you will stand out with an authentic value proposition! People will remember you and most importantly, they will **trust** you.

Finally, by creating a value proposition, you can mitigate nervousness. If you're one of the many people who get nervous and uncomfortable meeting and talking to people you don't know, then creating a value proposition is your solution.

Once established, you can simply memorise your value proposition and practice it over and over again. Whenever you meet new people, you'll always have something to start the conversation with. You won't have to think what to say and worry about whether or not it's appropriate. Internalising your value proposition will boost your confidence and increase your chances of leaving a lasting impression.

To sum it all up, being yourself and knowing how to communicate your value proposition is all it takes!

If you're ready, let's go!

6 Simple Steps to Your Highly Effective Personal Brand

Before we get started with defining your value proposition, we first need to look at two hard truths:

1. **Find a niche:** You can't be everything to everyone!

We need to find your sweet spot, the spot where you and your brand will be most successful. The spot in which you're so unique that no one can ignore you!

To find out out where that sweet spot is, we need to find the intersection between what you stand for, what you bring to the table and what the market needs. That's your opportunity niche, or the 'opportunity sweet spot' as I call it.

Why are we doing that? Because **you cannot be everything to everyone.** Highlight your uniqueness, that's what makes you different.

2. **Be active**: No one is waiting for you!

No one is searching for you. It's your job to make yourself seen and recognisable.

Let's say you're a software engineer who wants to start a tech blog. You might have a vast knowledge on various technologies, the necessary writing skills to bring new information to 'paper', and maybe even some sense of how to market your blog.

Ok, the problem with this example is that many other people have the same skills. As hard as it sounds, having the skills is the minimum requirement to make your aspirations work. They do not set you apart from anyone yet. At least not significantly. That's why you need to find your opportunity sweet spot.

And that spot is at the intersection where your values, your inner motivations and beliefs tie in together with your skills and the needs of the market.

If it were easy to find this unique opportunity sweet spot, everyone would have a powerful brand. It's not easy, but that's why I have created this simple step-by-step process to get you there.

I call this the Ladder to Uniqueness, or the secret to highly effective personal brands. The secret to this approach, and the reason I call it the ladder, is the steps included in this process and the order in which they should be completed. To create a powerful personal brand, you need a solid foundation and motivation. You should never skip a step or deviate from the prescribed order. If you follow this process, it's like climbing a ladder. You need a foundation and a wall to put and lean the ladder on (comprised of your goal and motivation, respectively) and to avoid falling down, you need to climb the ladder step by step. That's the secret! Working your way through this process one step at a time will allow you to create a strong, powerful and unique personal brand that gets you results – I promise. Just follow along, it's easier than it sounds.

That being said, let's take a look at the six steps that lie ahead of us:

1. Set goals
2. Define your values
3. Shape your image
4. Match your skills
5. Explore your added value
6. Discover your market fit

Stacked together, these steps create a unique and powerful brand with a strong foundation. A unique and highly effective personal brand that is built for success!

Step 1: Setting Goals for a Powerful Value Proposition

In the previous chapters, we discussed the importance of creating a value proposition when building a highly effective brand. That's why all of the steps and the following activities target the development of a value proposition, starting with your goal!

Before you can start walking up that ladder and build a personal brand, you need to know where and what your ladder of uniqueness points to. That point is your goal.

There are various goals to consider when creating your brand's value proposition.

1. **Why** do you want to have a personal brand?
2. **What** do you want to achieve with your personal brand?
3. **Who** do you want to address with your brand? Why them? What is the goal here?

This last question is particularly important. Are you addressing multiple target groups with the same personal brand?

Let's say you're a software engineer and career-wise you want to brand yourself as an expert for a certain engineering domain and/or coding language. But on the side you're working as a successful freelance photographer. For this side business you want to brand yourself as a creative, detail-oriented photographer who captures unique life events.

The value set is the same, obviously, since it's the same person (let's just say this software engineer is dedicated, detail-oriented and focused), but the goal of the value proposition is different. There's a different motivation, different skill set and above all a different target group behind both value propositions.

This example should illustrate how important it is to not skip the step of goal setting. It's vital to define a clear and convincing messaging afterwards.

But let's take this step by step.

Setting Goals With the GROW Model

One of the most powerful ways to define goals was created in 1992 by the world-famous performance coach Sir John Whitmore. The basic idea of the GROW model is to define achievable goals by taking the initial goal idea through a four stage process. At the end, you will have a goal that is actionable, practical and achievable.

These are the four steps:

1. **Goal**: What do you want to do? - Set a desired goal.
2. **Reality**: Where are you right now? - Explore your current status.
3. **Options**: How can you reach your goal? - Find appropriate courses of action.
4. **Will**: What will you do? - Make yourself accountable for what needs to be done, when and by whom.

Before diving into it, let's look at an example.

Let's say you're an aspiring social media influencer. Your goal as an influencer may be to reach 10K followers within the next three months and to create a convincing brand image that makes it easier to achieve that **(Goal)**. Now, let's do a reality check. What's the current follower count? Your profile shows that you've collected 2.000 followers over the course of one year **(Reality)**. Next, you must think about how you can acquire 8.000 more followers four times faster. You can organize give-aways, spend a few hours per day posting content and increasing your engagement. You could also host account takeovers with other aspiring influencers and much more **(Options)**. Lastly, grab your weekly planner or calendar and make a timeline. On which day will you do what? How much time do you need to spend and where will these tasks fit into your day? **(Will)**

Once you've gone through the entire process, pause, take a step back and assess your goal. Is it achievable? Be brutally honest with yourself. Will you really be able to stick to the timeline and schedule? Is there a chance that you'll give up or get sloppy with your tasks halfway?

If yes, go back to the process included in stage four and rethink your goal. The purpose of a goal is to achieve it. There's no point in running after a goal you already know will overwhelm you. It will only demotivate you and eventually cause you to neglect the project. Let's avoid that outcome at all costs!

A good goal is SMART, PURE and CLEAR

In addition to the GROW framework, there are three more approaches that help you refine a very broad goal to an achievable one. These goal setting approaches are called SMART, PURE and CLEAR. You can download a worksheet for SMART goals to help you complete this task.

But here's what these words mean in terms of goal setting:

SMART =	PURE =	CLEAR =
Specific	**P**ositive	**C**hallenging
Measurable	**U**nderstood	**L**egal
Achievable	**R**elevant	**E**nvironmentally sound
Realistic	**E**thical	**A**ppropriate
Timebound		**R**ecorded

Keep these three frameworks in mind when moving forward. Here are a few questions that will help you define a powerful goal.

PRACTICE EXERCISES

The following exercises are also available in a worksheet format on melaniegoel.com.

Goal

1. What goal and purpose should your brand support?
2. What outcome do you want to reach with your brand?
3. How personally invested are you in this goal? Are you invested in keeping your brand aligned with this goal?
4. How can you rephrase this goal so that it depends exclusively on you and not on others?
5. When will you know that you've achieved the goal - how will you measure your success?
6. When will you have reached your goal?

Reality

1. What's your current progress on this goal (i.e. what's the current follower count, knowledge on a certain topic etc.)?
2. Do you already have some kind of brand messaging associated with your goal?
3. What have you already accomplished with this goal?
4. Who else is involved in achieving your goal, and how? Are you dependent on someone?
5. What have you tried already? What impact did those actions have?
6. What accounts for the gap between you today and your goal? What is missing? Are you the person who can close the gap?
7. Does your desired brand align with the goal?
8. Do your values align with the goal?

Options

1. What could you do about your goal, current situation and the gap in between?

2. How can your brand help you achieve this goal?
3. What does your brand need to be more successful in achieving this goal?
4. What other potential courses of action can you think of? Try to think of at least 5 potential activities.
5. List all the things you've done already. What else is there?
6. Who could help you?
7. What have others done that might also work for you?

Will

1. Which option/s do you want to pursue? Which ones are most likely to lead to success?
2. What will you do and by when?
3. What step(s) could you take today to move forward?
4. On a scale of one to ten, how likely is it that you will get your tasks done in the set time frame?
5. Which potential obstacles do you need to address to make sure the tasks get done?

The last step is by far the most difficult one to follow through on but I've got you covered here as well. In the last chapter, I will share a few tested techniques with you that will help you stick to your goals and schedule.

Where Your Personal Brand Meets Your Goal

Let's look at an example to highlight how your goal and your personal brand fit together.

To do so, I would like to introduce you to someone who'll be by your side throughout the book from now on: Fictional Pete. Fictional Pete is a tech blogger from New York. In his tech reviews, he eliminates all marketing verbiage. The reason he does this is because he wants to help people, particularly those who aren't tech people themselves, understand what technologies really can and cannot do. So, let's see what an achievable goal would look like for him and how it aligns with his personal brand.

Grow: I want to increase my mailing list by 3K subscribers within the next 6 months (timebound, measurable, specific, realistic and achievable).

Reality: As of today, I acquired 5K subscribers within 12 months by posting on Twitter, Reddit and other platforms. I've done guest posts and appeared in a few podcasts to increase awareness.

Options: I could do advertising, buying slots in newsletters etc.; I could also try and get in touch with more successful bloggers and ask them to give my blog a shout out; I could create a consistent brand image for my blog to position it as the place to go for no-bullshit tech reviews, this will help me create word of mouth publicity and get recognized.

Will: I work fulltime on this blog and am willing to put in extra hours to achieve my goal. I'm also willing to invest $1.000 to achieve this goal within 6 months.

Your personal brand is a means to reach your goal. It's not the only means, but it is one of the most powerful. Another means is advertising. The great thing about advertising is that it gives you a quick start and instant gratification. Something you won't get from personal branding. However, just think for a second about how much money you can really spend? At some point you'd like your brand to run without spending money, right? The thing is, once you stop running ads, your performance will most likely drop significantly. You've spent money on ads, got some new customers in return, but that's it. But why stop there?

Advertising without branding is like using disposable utensils. You use it, you get something out of it and you throw it away. It's not sustainable and it is incredibly expensive. If you have the means to invest in advertising, do it sustainably. Go the extra mile and create a personal brand first. Then promote your brand in ads and across all of the other activities that you do. With that approach, people will continue to recognize you even after you've stopped putting out ads. Whatever you do, the goal should be to plant your brand image in the mind of your audience and get continuously recognized. Regardless of which marketing strategies you use to get there, they will work best if you have a consistent brand in place.

How do you feel after this exercise? Did you get more clarity on your goal(s) and why they're important? If so, please continue defining your values in the next chapter. However, if you'd like to spend more time on the goal setting exercises and want some help refining your results, then check out some of my blogs and videos. It's important to nail this step because it's the foundation for your ladder. If you put your ladder on a wobbly surface, it'll fall and crash.

Step 2: Defining Values

Imagine you come across a business owner whose company sells sustainable goods. The entire brand is focused on eco-friendly, climate-conservation and waste-reducing rhetoric and imagery. Suddenly, you find out that it was all fake. The company, the owner, their message, products - absolutely everything was greenwashed. None of it was real, it was just a marketing strategy to generate more profit.

How would that make you feel? How would that affect your trust in the brand? How would it affect your willingness to buy from them? For me, this company would lose me as a customer immediately, regardless of how good their intentions or marketing may be. Building a brand takes time and effort, but it takes just a few seconds to destroy it. If you build your brand on fake values, it's as fragile as a domino in a domino game.

Values are the foundation of your brand. They are the wall your ladder leans against and the material your ladder is made of. Without values, a brand has no direction, appears incoherent and fragile. Without honest values, your personal brand lacks authenticity. Authenticity supplies your uniqueness factor, therefore brands without authenticity have no chance of standing out today. The more authentic your values are, the more unique your personal brand will be.

Why is it then that so few companies, business owners, influencers and side project hustlers think about their values before they start out? For one, it takes courage to find out what you stand for. It requires patience because branding doesn't pay off immediately. This is tricky to accept, particularly in the beginning when you want to see progress. It can also be scary because once you define your authentic values, you start limiting your target group. Your individual values may not appeal to everyone and, unfortunately, trying to be everything to everyone is one of the biggest branding mistakes. It's scary, I totally get it. But if you build a brand that is authentic to you, you already know who is receptive to your brand messaging: people who you already interact and get along with. People who are in your life because they value you for who you are. Find people who are similar and that's your most receptive target group.

Knowing this makes everything easier along the way. Narrowing your target group and giving up control in this area is extremely difficult, but it pays off. I promise! However, I don't want to go too far on this topic right now, because we'll discuss target groups in more detail later in the book.

Before we really dig into this topic, let's look at Pete for one last example of why choosing authentic values is so important.

Create momentum by being authentic

Although Pete is a quiet, analytical person, he continued to observe that extroverts are more successful than him. So, he decided to act more extroverted in order to achieve what others achieved. This went well for some time but was extremely exhausting. With time, he forgot to 'act' like an extrovert and got increasingly frustrated with faking his personality. Eventually, he dropped the act and left people feeling very confused about the change in his behavior. What was real, what was fake? Why did he feel like he had to act like someone he's not? Is a person like that even trustworthy? If he's faking things just to get ahead, probably not.

Do you see what happened here? The bottom line is that you'll confuse, disappoint and maybe even lose people who bought into your act if you don't remain authentic. No one wants to be betrayed or lied to and they'll stop trusting you as a result, especially if they find out that you pretended to be something you are not just to get something they have.

This is a harsh example but it resembles what many of us do all the time. We tell people that we are X, even though we're Y, just because we believe it'll increase our chances to get that job, that promotion, that investor deal, that partner... How often did that work out successfully in the long-run?

I really want to emphasize this here before we get into the exercises because if you go with anything other than the authentic values that come naturally to you at this stage, there's a good chance that you will have to repeat the entire branding process again in a few months.

So, let's utilize time efficiently and go through this process correctly right from the start.

What Are Values?

I've been quite blunt on the last few pages but personal branding is about being honest with yourself. It's also about answering extremely tough questions. I really want you to finish reading this book feeling that you've had an 'Aha' moment and that your time was well spent. To make that happen, it's my job as a brand consultant to show you where so many others have made their mistakes, so that you can avoid them. No one ever made progress with sugar-coated advice.

So, before you set out to define your authentic values, have you ever asked yourself what values actually are? Have you considered what your values say about you and why is it so hard to define them?

I remember when I started learning all about personal branding 4 years ago. I really struggled with the question of what values are. Even more frustrating was answering the question: 'What do I stand for?'. I was so overwhelmed by the fact that I couldn't answer those questions that I went into complete denial and simply refused to think about them. But, in the back of my mind I heard a voice constantly asking: 'Shouldn't I know who I am and what I live for? Why can others answer these questions but I have no clue?'. So, I literally started from the bottom; I opened a dictionary and looked up the term 'values'. There were a ton of different results, and one really resonated with me.

Dictionary to the rescue

Let's take a look at that definition here: "principles or standards of behavior; one's judgement of what is important in life" (www.lexico.com) At first, this definition looked quite technical and not particularly useful to me, so I tried to make sense of it by going through the definition word by word. Let's take a good look at this definition together, it's more fun that way!

Principles/Standards

> **Principles or standards** *of behavior;*
> *one's judgement of what is important in life.*

Reading these two words was the first breakthrough for me. Although I had a hard time defining my values, I found it easier to identify my principles. Why? A friend and practicing therapist taught me a trick: Just think about everything that makes you upset and angry. In these situations, it's very likely that one of your principles was violated either by yourself or by someone else. For example, I get very upset when I see plastic litter outside. It contradicts my principles of protecting our planet, looking out for my fellow humans and not being ignorant and selfish.

Each of us has principles. Our principles consist of what we think makes an experience good or bad, ethical or unethical, or even what we consider to be a rewarding or disappointing life. Our principles shape what we think is worth spending our time, money or effort on. They help us make decisions that bring us closer to living a life we deem important, a life we **value**.

PRACTICE QUESTIONS

1. What upsets you in daily life? List 3-5 things.
2. What do you feel really strongly about in life - positively & negatively?

Behavior

Principles or standards of **behavior**;
one's judgement of what is important in life.

The questions you just answered lead us to the next chunk of the definition of 'behavior'. Importantly, principles are only principles if they're put into action. Otherwise, they're nothing but empty phrases. The more you practice putting your principles into action, the sooner this behavior will become a habit. At some point, your desired behavior will become so internalized that you will start living according to your principles without making much (if any) effort.

Stephen Covey, author of the bestselling 'The 7 Habits of Highly Effective People', describes principles as a "natural law".

Natural law is a theory in ethics and philosophy that says that human beings possess intrinsic values that govern our reasoning and behavior. Natural law maintains that these rules of right and wrong are inherent in people and are not created by society or court judges.*

What does that mean for you? Well, it means that you have values, and principles for that matter, that are truly yours and independent of others. Those values determine what you find worthwhile and valuable. Therefore, to find out what those values are, you need to look inward instead of outward. You need to listen to yourself, your inner voice and find out what makes you tick.

Knowing which intrinsic values govern your actions and decision-making is a super-power. Once you know this, you can utilize those values to their fullest potential not just to build a highly effective brand, but to get you what you want. Why? If you know who you are and which values drive you, you will get a pretty clear idea of what you want. It is something very few people know and the main reason they run after everything and nothing at the same time only to end up being less successful. That's why getting clarity on who you are and what you want makes you more effective, dedicated and focused!

PRACTICE QUESTIONS

1. What kind of life would you like to think back on in old age?
2. What do you need to practice every single day to make that life happen **now**?

Judgement

Principles or standards of behavior;
one's judgement *of what is important in life.*

If principles are natural laws that shape your behaviour and if those natural laws mean that deep inside we inherently know what's right and what's wrong, then why are we so scared of making decisions? We are scared because we don't seem to know what is the right or wrong thing to do.

Because we unlearned listening to that inner voice that's governed by natural laws. Most of us aren't aware of our values and we aren't aware of that inherent judgement system. We get confused between what we want and what others think and more often than not, we decide in favor of the latter. We excessively overthink situations, because we're unsure who to please - ourselves or others? And unfortunately along the way while blending in, we forget who to listen to. But have no fear! I will show you how you can re-learn to listen to that inner voice and your natural laws with an exercise inspired by the transformative coach Michael Neill.

PRACTICE EXERCISE

In this exercise, you will analyse your behavior to determine if it aligns with your values or not. Although we have yet to define what your values are, this exercise will help you identify them. So, to get started, think of a situation in which you were confused by your own behaviour. It doesn't matter if the situation was serious or inconsequential.

Now, take a coin. In a moment I will ask you to flip it. Once you flip and while it's still rotating, you decide which side corresponds with 'This behaviour was not ok' and which one with 'This behaviour represents me.' You have a split-second to do this. Are you ready? Now, flip the coin. In one second, the universe will determine whether your behavior was good or bad. (Just for fun, what's your gut feeling about which answer is true?) Now, the moment of truth has arrived. What does the coin say? And how do you feel about the result? Relieved? Queasy? What was your gut feeling? Whatever the answer, your gut feeling is your natural law, that often overlooked inner voice. Did your mind say that your behavior was okay, but your gut indicated something different? Your gut's signal is often the real and honest answer that aligns with your deeper principles and values.

Why do we neglect this voice so often? Well, sometimes that voice tells us things that we don't **want** to hear. Often it forces us to admit our own mistakes.

That's why this exercise is so powerful. This exercise is brutally honest. Basically, it allows you to be brutally honest with yourself. And never forget that everyone makes mistakes. So don't be too hard on yourself. Mistakes come and go. If you can, embrace this exercise as a catalyst for you to build a personal brand that is aligned with your authentic values and to be more conscious of what your values are on a daily basis. A good rule of thumb is to listen to your inner voice before your mind second-guesses it. No one said that's easy, but the reward is long-term, specifically, a more satisfying life and a more powerful brand.

What Is Important in Life

Principles or standards of behavior;
one's judgement of **what is important in life.**

Why do you need to know what's important to you in life before creating a brand? How does defining your judgement and values benefit your brand? Why make all this effort? If you create a personal brand, the brand is about you. It is **personal**. And if you want to convince someone that you are worthy of their attention, you first need to be convinced yourself. You need to be convinced of the 'me' you're promoting.

To stand out, you need to know what you stand for

This doesn't just apply to personal brands. That also applies to side projects and any product for which your personality may increase the rate of success. Simply said, before you put yourself out there, you need to decide how you want to be perceived. And whatever the answer is, it should align with who you truly are. Your values, your principles and what you think is important in life. This is crucial because when the service or product you are promoting aligns with who you really are and not a fake persona, you've created an authentic brand experience. And this matters because authentic brand experiences are powerful, engaging and pull people in.

Authenticity Is the Key

If you want your brand to be successful, you must do this foundational work and really get into the nitty-gritty of who you are, what motivates you and what you value in life. If you followed along and completed the previous exercises, you probably already have a clearer idea of your values. Let's finally start working with your values then.

PRACTICE EXERCISE

Write down all the answers from the previous questions on a piece of paper (feel free to do this on paper or on your computer).

The previous questions:

1. What upsets you in daily life?
2. What do you feel really strongly about in life - positively & negatively?
3. What kind of life would you want to think back on in old age? What do you need to do every single day to make that life happen?
4. Which principles and values did your gut tell you are important to you?

Now, download the personal brand values worksheet from my website. Highlight **10** of the 150 values that resonate with you the most. Next, try to prioritise the selected values based on their importance to you (the first being the most important) and how much each value influences your daily decision-making (the first being the most influential).

Take all your answers from the questions above and the values worksheet and see if you can identify a pattern. Is there a theme throughout your answers? Can you identify one or two values that continue to appear? If so, write them down and say them out loud. How do you feel when you hear those values? Do you feel proud? Liberated? Do they feel authentic to you? Would your family and friends associate you with those values?

Value-Oriented Habits Make You More Authentic and Successful

Values and Goals

In the previous chapter, we talked extensively about the art of setting achievable but challenging goals. We went through the GROW methodology and learned that goals should always be SMART, PURE and CLEAR.

To summarize: Well-defined goals are time-bound and measurable. These features serve as benchmarks that allow us to track our progress. This gives us the opportunity to get a real sense of achievement, or lets us know that we need to put in more effort. Also, goals are naturally future-oriented because they are linked to the desire to accomplish something in the future. A goal is complete once the targeted outcome has been reached.

Values on the other hand are very different from goals. Values never end. They're not time-bound or particularly measurable. Values give direction and exist in the present. They guide your daily actions and give you a sense of what's right and what's wrong. Moreover, a value is not an achievement in itself. Values are highly subjective. While you may perceive one value as positive, someone else may see the same value as negative. Or, a value can be positive in a certain setting but is negative in another. We could say, either you **have** a specific value or your goal is to **acquire** the value. That's the difference between goals and values. For the latter scenario you would create a time-bound, achievable goal process that will allow you to measure and assess your success in internalizing that value.

> *The goal is the acquisition of a value, not the value itself*

To help you visualize the difference between values and goals, let me tell you a story about myself and the progress of writing this ebook.

I've struggled with staying consistent with personal projects in the past. I tend to let myself get distracted by the things happening around me like my phone buzzing, my dog barking, the postman ringing, my friends inviting me on a coffee date, my family calling, and the list goes on. No matter how committed I was to achieving a goal, I prioritized the 'easier' tasks and started to get sloppy on the 'harder' tasks that would actually help me reach that goal. Once I got sloppy, it was nearly impossible to jump back on the bandwagon. I usually gave up on my project and felt disappointed and disheartened. This time, while writing this ebook, I wanted to do things differently. With every fiber of my body I wanted to stick to a daily writing routine, no matter what happened around me.

The goal was to acquire and strengthen the value of consistency in my life

This is exactly how I framed my goal: I want to write an ebook by October 2020. In order to achieve this, I need to strengthen the value of consistency and stick to my daily writing routine. The next question you might already be asking yourself is, *how did I get there?*

Values and Habits

I realised that I needed to create habits that **resembled the value** but **pointed towards the goal**. I had to change something about the way I approached my previous project goals. Essentially, I had to internalize the habit of doing something that would help me achieve my goal and I had to make arrangements that would make it easy for me to stay consistent.

The easier it is to maintain a habit, the more likely you are to follow through

Like James Clear, author of the International Bestseller 'Atomic Habits', wrote: 'Changing our habits is challenging for two reasons: (1) we try to change the wrong thing and (2) we try to change our habits in the wrong way.'

Usually, when we pursue a goal, we simply write down the list of tasks that once achieved will get us there, like 'doing X will result in Y'. James Clear calls that an 'outcome-based habit'. However, that didn't really work for me (and according to Clear's research it doesn't work for most people either). He advocates a concept called 'identity-based habits' instead. So, what does that mean? An identity-based habit entails you trying to **personally identify** with your goal instead of seeing it as a 'thing to be achieved'. Once you've done that, you then make small incremental steps every single day to improve the habits that will eventually get you to your goal. This is best illustrated with an example. Let's again take the example of me writing this book. Remember the way I framed the goal before? I said: 'I want to write an ebook by October 2020. In order to achieve that I need to strengthen the value of consistency and stick to my daily writing routine.' As you can see, the way the goal is framed here makes it difficult to become personally invested. So, let's try to reframe it so that it's more about me and my identity:

> I'm a writer. I'm the kind of writer who is disciplined about writing every day to produce an ebook that will help thousands of people create and shape their personal brand.

How powerful is this?! We just nailed the value part of my desired habit. Now, the value becomes part of my identity. And I wouldn't want to let myself down, would I? So, I started to stick with it.

Creating Small Value-Based Habits

This is a crucial step. I've mentioned that a personal brand is most powerful when you completely identify with the image you're creating as your brand.

Your brand's authenticity stems from your values and is evidenced by your actions. If you live value-based habits, your actions will naturally align with your brand and make it authentic and powerful.

But how can you create those habits and how will they help you achieve your goals? Improve whatever you're doing by incorporating the desired value a tiny bit every day!

PRACTICE EXERCISE

1. Think of the brand image you want to create.
2. Next, use one of the goals you set in the previous chapter.

3. Now, define what's currently missing between today's status and your goal. Which value do you need to internalize to reach your goal?

Example: **Consistency**

4. List everything that could potentially keep you from living according to that value and reaching the desired goal. Write full sentences describing what those items are. This will help your brain understand and internalize the barriers.

Example: **I cannot be consistent because I get distracted too easily.**

5. Take all of the items in the list and dig deeper. What is it about these things that keeps you from working on your goal? Be as specific as possible.

Example: **I cannot be consistent because I'm too distracted by my phone buzzing, I have no dedicated workspace, my back hurts...**

6. Now, do the same thing again. Take those items and dig even deeper. Get to the root cause of what is keeping you from reaching your goal. Insert each of your items into this template sentence:

Example: **I cannot be consistent because my chair is so uncomfortable that I get distracted by my back pain whenever I sit for longer than 2 hours.**

7. Now that you've identified all the root causes, you can begin looking for solutions to improve them.

Example: **Buy a new chair.**

You need goals so that you know where you're going but to really achieve your goal, you need to eliminate the root causes of your previous failures. There's a reason people say: Fail fast and learn from it. This is the situation where you can apply everything you've learned. Take the time to understand why you weren't already able to get to where you wanted to go, dig deep and find the root causes. From there, start improving your processes and habits based on your values. Keep questioning them: Are my habits aligned with my values? Are they taking me where I want to go?

Improving Your Value-Based Habits

While writing this book, I realised that my habits weren't aligned with my values and therefore, they limited my success.

1. My environment was unproductive: My desk was in the living room facing the window, with lots of stuff on it. I sat on a kitchen chair and had a bright external monitor. To make matters worse, my desk was close to the kitchen and my home's main entrance. There was so much distraction caused by the temptation to eat or the disturbance caused by someone ringing the bell.
2. I had no strict daily schedule: I used to loosely write down my daily tasks in a notebook. This helped me keep track of what I needed to do, but it didn't make me stick to my agenda. I just crossed the items off and transferred them over to the next day. Not particularly effective.
3. I wasn't personally invested: I realized that my lack of dedication and consistency also came from the lack of honest investment. I did not identify 100% with the goal and the tasks at hand. I did not make it part of my identity.

Now, let's take a look at what has changed, otherwise you wouldn't be reading this book today.

I actually started keeping a habit book. I defined which values (for me these were consistency and dedication) I wanted to internalize. Then I started my first new habit: before going to sleep, I write down one habit that I want to improve. Next, I changed my work environment. I turned my desk so that it faced the wall, I bought an ergonomic chair, I turned off my (secondary) monitor every time I wrote, and I tidied up my desk every evening after I finished working. I then created the aforementioned identity-based value statement, printed it out and pasted it next to my monitor. Now, I'm reminded every morning that I'm a consistent writer.

I'm a writer. I'm the kind of writer who consistently writes every day to create an ebook that will help thousands of people build and shape their personal brand.

However, I didn't have a solution for what would best help me stick to my writing schedule. So, I tried a new approach. I took out my list of 10 values and noticed that one of those values was reliability. And an important aspect of reliability is being punctual. So, if I needed a strategy to help me stick to something, why not create an artificial environment in which I had to be punctual? There it was - my strategy! I carved out time slots just for writing and scheduled them as meetings in my Google calendar. Getting a notification about an upcoming meeting with myself and my writing program did the trick simply because I went back to my values to remind myself of what makes me tick. Of course, just because this strategy worked for me does not mean that it's going to work for you. But with this example in mind, think about which of your core values has the power to make you stick to something? How could you utilize this value to come up with a solution?

Take some time to think about the best way. As I said before, values and habits are subjective. What works for one person, won't necessarily work for another. But don't skip this essential step because this is the step that will anchor you to your goal.

Value-based habits are the core foundation of a powerful personal brand. Remember? You can talk a lot, but your actions are what people will remember. If they don't align with your value proposition, your audience won't take you seriously.

The Difference Between Personal Values and Brand Values

If you've been following along and have downloaded the personal brand values worksheet, you now have a wide selection of values at your disposal to inspire you on your journey to create a personal brand. However, values are subjective and while one value may be positive for some people, the same value may be negative for you. Similarly, the positive or negative nature of a value may be determined by the setting.

Let's say you value creativity and you brand yourself as someone who finds creative solutions. Some people will choose you because they love that 'out-of-the-box' angle, others might decide against you because creativity scares them. Perhaps the latter prefers the ordinary because it seems safer. Neither of these responses is wrong. People are different. Just as you and I are different. Understanding and accepting this fundamental truth is important. We can't make everyone happy. And we can't be everything to everyone. That being said, the values of the person behind a personal brand are the brand's values. However, you can always choose to highlight some of your values more than others in your personal brand.

Let's look at our tech blogger, Fictional Pete, again. His personal values are fairness, accuracy, service, simplicity, diligence, analysis and honesty. These values guide Fictional Pete through life and help him make the right decisions. But, Pete doesn't want to highlight all his personal values in his personal brand because they don't all seem relevant to the promotion of his tech blog. Pete decides to focus on accuracy, simplicity, diligence, analysis and honesty because those are the values that will build the backbone of his personal brand and his value proposition.

So, when you decide which of your values to include in your brand image, focus on the ones that are authentic to you and simultaneously serve your goal.

Avoid the Branding Trap

Now is a good time to explain why I keep repeating myself about authenticity. The simple reason is that very few brands take this part seriously and, eventually, wonder why they fail.

What happens most of the time is that we come across someone's account, website, product and so on and we like what that person is doing. Let's say we're even impressed by them. So, we decide to copy what they're doing, putting more and more effort into creating an image that is similar to theirs. At some point, we get frustrated because we don't end up being as successful as them. This is what I call the branding trap! And here's my tip: Don't go there!

Let's deconstruct the entire process.

Why were you attracted to that person's profile, product, etc.? What about it impressed you? Were you impressed by their vision, their expertise, their skills, their lifestyle? If your answer to any of these is yes, then this person did a good job branding themselves. But what we need to understand is that it is *their* vision, *their* expertise, *their* skill and *their* lifestyle, not yours. No two people are the same. Even if you have a similar mindset and/or skill set as another person, the two of you are not the same. It will be extremely difficult to reproduce *their* success. And that's a good thing, because you bring other unique traits to the table. And that uniqueness is your key to success!

Your personality. *Your* individual experience. *Your* character. Use these!

You can build a similar product, influencer profile, blog and so on, but merely copying someone else's won't work. Include yourself, your values and your personality and you'll see a positive effect on your brand.

PRACTICE QUESTIONS

1. What do you want your brand to stand for?
2. Which of your values do you want to shine through in your brand?
3. Which of your traits should your clients know about?

Woohoo! You've climbed another step on the Ladder to Uniqueness. The step 'values' is complete. Do you feel confident about your choice in values? Are you ready to continue and build your brand image? Then I'll see you in the next chapter. There's lots of awesome stuff coming your brand's way!

Step 3: Shaping Your Image

Now that we have two steps behind us, are you ready for the third one? So far, you've set goals for your brand and defined your values. The two foundational steps are done. Now you have a solid foundation to put and lean your ladder on. Still, it doesn't feel like a brand yet, does it? We have loose information about who you are, but not a unified picture of what your brand will look like. That's why in this chapter, we're going to combine all of this information to form a proper brand image. Upon completing this step, you will have a good sense of your brand image. You will know what your brand purpose is, and what your brand voice and brand message look like. You'll also get an initial sense of what a unified, authentic brand feels like. Ready? Then let's get started!

Brand Purpose

In the introduction to branding, I presented what a brand purpose is and what it does for your personal brand.

Here's a brief reminder:

A **brand purpose** is the WHY of your brand. It highlights the human element of a brand. It makes it easy for your audience to connect with you on an emotional level and to identify with your personality and your values.

That means, the brand purpose is your chance to connect with your audience on an emotional level. This matters because it is at this level that you can leave a meaningful first impression and create a memorable experience for your customers. It makes your personal brand, in other words, you, more relatable. If people can personally identify with your brand, they are more likely to pay more attention to what you have to say. That's why your brand purpose is also your way to get your foot in the door.

Before asking you to answer this section's practice questions, I'd like to ask you to remember the authenticity rule. Don't look outward. Don't search for the purposes you think people might be interested in. First, look inward and rest assured that there's a target group that will resonate with your brand purpose.

The brand purpose is the emotional gateway to your audience.
It absolutely MUST be authentic.

Why? Why is the question of the day! Your brand purpose is entirely based on the question why. Why are you doing what you're doing?

Are you feeling a bit overwhelmed by this question? You're not alone. It's a hard one. We're so busy with our idea, or the goal we want to achieve, be it positioning ourselves to get promoted, taking photos to get more engagement, or writing blog content to get traction, that we totally forget why we're doing what we're doing. We forget the big picture.

Be honest, did you ask yourself why you're doing this? Why do you want to get promoted? What makes you work so hard to get that promotion? Why do you want to become an influencer? What drives you to do that? Why do you want to provide tech content to your audience? What drives you to invest all of this time? Think beyond money and more in terms of your inner convictions. No one asked you to do this, so why are you?

Let me illustrate this question with one of my own examples. Why did I quit my well-paid, secure job to become a personal brand strategist? Why did I sit down for five hours every day for a month to write this book?

I believe that every single person should have the same opportunities. People have told me that that's idealistic, but it's my inner conviction. I adopt dogs (and would love to adopt a kid), because I believe that everyone deserves a fair chance. So, I quit my job because I saw that people with incredible talent and potential had a hard time positioning themselves and consequently missed out on life-changing opportunities. By sharing my knowledge, I want to help these people fulfil their potential and succeed in whatever way they aspire to. Making money along the way is essential, yes, but it's not my motivation. It's not what drives me. It's not what made me sit down for hours every day. What drove me was the urge to share my knowledge as soon as possible, so that I can start making a difference.

That's my brand purpose. That's my emotional connection to you, my audience. This is the aspect that makes me relatable and approachable. And it's authentic. It's a purpose that comes natural to me. But now, what about you?

PRACTICE QUESTIONS

1. What motivates you?
2. What drives you to do what you're doing?
3. What is essential to you?
4. What are you trying to achieve with this brand?
5. If you had only one thing you could communicate, what would you want people to know about you?
6. What's your purpose in life?

Collect your answers and identify a pattern. Which motivators are similar across all your answers? If you find a commonality (like in my case **sharing knowledge in order to enable everyone to succeed**) then say it out loud. How does it make you feel? Are you proud to associate yourself with this purpose? If yes, awesome! You have found your personal brand purpose! In other words, the gateway to your audience. If what you've uncovered does not resonate with you, look at your answers again and try to find the one purpose that fills you with pride, joy and motivation.

Are you feeling good about your selection now? Then let's continue developing a brand voice (also called tone of voice) that resembles your brand values and purpose.

Brand Voice

In this chapter, we will develop your brand's tone of voice or brand voice. But let's first take a look at what that actually is:

A **tone of voice** defines how your brand communicates with your audience and influences how people experience your messaging. Your tone of voice represents your brand's personality and values.

To be honest, many years ago, before I got into branding, I thought that tone of voice was a weird concept. How can a 'thing', like a brand, have a voice. But through my experiences, I learned that a brand voice is absolutely essential. It's one of the elements that distinguishes you in the market. The best way to get to a brand tone of voice is to apply a persona. For a personal brand, this is easy, because the applied persona is yours. Allow me to demonstrate how you can go about applying your persona.

PRACTICE EXERCISE

First, write down the values that you want to be associated with your brand. Then, add the brand purpose from the previous section to your list.

Next, decide how a person with that identity, purpose and value set would communicate. Here's a visualization to help you with this: Imagine two people meet on the street. One of them is your brand identity, the other is your ideal audience. How would your brand identity approach that person? What communication style would your brand identity use?

Let's say you're Fictional Pete and you want to promote an analytical, straightforward tech blogger identity. Your brand purpose is to write tech reviews without confusing marketing jargon and present your audience with useful facts about trending technologies. What kind of words would someone like that use? How long would the posts of such a person be? What kind of imagery would you use? What kind of writing style would correspond to that identity? Would such a person communicate in a reserved, professional, colloquial, or easy-going tone? Is that person loud, quiet, introverted, or extroverted?

Before we analyze Pete's case, here's a reminder of his values: fairness, **accuracy**, service, **simplicity**, **diligence**, **analysis** and **honesty** (the values in bold should be highlighted in his personal brand).

If you were Pete, you might decide that a persona with your values would write blog articles that are **analytical** and straight to the point without excessive language because you're promoting a no-nonsense image (based on honesty and accuracy). Consequently, your articles will be of medium length. To reinforce your desired image, you would probably also use a **simple** writing style. You might even employ moderate sarcasm while introducing particular technologies as 'nobullshit'.

While answering these questions, always keep your values in mind. Your answers about how your persona, and eventually your brand identity, communicates should align with the values you want to promote, just as they did in the exercise above.

The brand tone of voice is also one of the best examples of why authenticity is so important. If you choose values that are inauthentic, you are prone to mess up your communication. A simple test to check whether you stayed authentic with your branding is to look at your answers from the previous exercise regarding how your persona would communicate. How does that persona communicate differently to how you communicate today? Do those two communication styles deviate from one another? If the answer is yes, maybe go back and double-check whether or not you've chosen a communication style that aligns with your values.

That being said, before you finalize your tone of voice, take a look outward. What does a target group that identifies with a brand voice like what you've come up with look like? You don't have to do a target group analysis just yet, we'll get there later; just try to first get a sense of where your voice fits. Do you have to dial down, or dial up?

If you have followed all of the exercises in this book until now, you shouldn't have too much tweaking to do here. All you need to do now whenever you plan an activity, is ask: 'Does this language/image etc. align with my values?' If yes, go ahead and produce that output. If no, change it. Make sure you ask yourself this question every time you create an output to ensure a consistent communication style.

Stay Consistent with Your Brand Voice

Your goal should be for people to recognize you across all forms of media you utilise to promote your personal brand. Wherever you're active with your brand, communicate consistently.

To demonstrate, I will give an example from my own personal brand journey. When I decided on the brand identity for my coaching business, I determined that my tone of voice and messaging will be conversational, colloquial and approachable. I want my audience to feel like they're talking to me while they're reading. Consequently, I wrote this book in a conversational style. I post content on LinkedIn, Twitter, Reddit and Instagram the exact same way. Similarly, I broadcast live videos in the same style. Basically, every single outward communication matches my brand identity. Why did I choose a conversational style? Because it comes naturally to me. I'm not a formal person and I don't like hierarchy. I want to engage people coactively. It's the most authentic way I can communicate, so I chose this style for my personal brand.

How does it feel to almost have your brand image ready? Do you feel it's coming together? Does it look like a coherent image to you? Take a moment to write down all of the elements of your brand. This includes your values, your persona or brand identity, your brand purpose and your brand voice. How does this make you feel? Do you feel represented by this image? Does it feel true to you?

By the way, if you're a visual learner, you may find it helpful to draw a persona and make a visual translation of everything you've created for your personal brand up until now.

Brand Message

Phew...how do you feel right now? Overwhelmed? Happy? Pumped? You've achieved so much already. Don't give up now, it'll be worth it!

Sometimes, I compare the first stages of branding with content marketing. Everyone knows it's crucial and that it's a long-term investment that pays off over time, but it's so hard to stick to because it doesn't give instant gratification or a sense of achievement. That's why it's a good idea to look back at your achievements whenever you feel like giving up. Those achievements might feel small or insignificant, but they're not. Every single one of them is a milestone on your journey to creating your personal brand and engineering long-term success. In order to keep you going, let's quickly look at your achievements.

By now, you've

1. set goals for your brand
2. defined your values in depth – who you are, what you stand for, what's important to you in life and more
3. visualized a brand identity persona
4. created a brand purpose
5. defined your brand voice (tone of voice)

Isn't that incredible? To finish off your brand image, we only need to work on one more thing: your brand messaging. After that it gets easier, I promise.

Introduce Your Brand and Leave Others Wanting More

The most important question to ask yourself when defining your messaging is: What do you want people to know about you? What's the first, second and third thing they need to know to get an idea of who you are, what you do and how they'll benefit from engaging with you.

An exercise that can help you define those answers more easily is the elevator pitch exercise. Imagine, you step inside an elevator with someone you want to impress, or any other person that is crucial to achieving your goal. You don't know how long that person will remain in the elevator, so you need to prioritize your messaging to get the most out of your time together.

The solution is something I call **brand message stacking**.

PRACTICE EXERCISE

Let's say the elevator takes 15 seconds to go from one floor to the next.

1. If you had only 15 seconds, what's the most essential information about your personal brand that the other person should hear before leaving the elevator?
2. If you had a second floor, what would you say next?
3. If you had one more floor, what's the third most important thing this person should know about you?
4. ... and so on.

I call this brand message stacking because you literally stack your messages on top of each other depending on how much time and attention you get. The most important and essential information must be said first and then you continue to add the next most important message on top. It's critical that you be strict with yourself and stick to 15 seconds when creating your pitch. There's a reason Instagram, TikTok and other social media, restrict their videos to 15 seconds. On average, 15 seconds is the maximum span of attention people will give you. During that time, people decide whether it's worth listening to you or not.

Before we get to an example, I want to quickly remind you not to forget about your brand purpose, value and brand voice while answering the questions above. We defined all three beforehand because they make up your messaging.

Let's see how our tech blogger Pete would go about this exercise. His values are diligence, analysis and honesty. His brand purpose is to remove the bullshit from tech marketing to explain what technologies are really about. His voice is modest, easy going, simple and sometimes sarcastic. What could his messaging sound like?

1. **First floor:** Hi there. Nice to meet you. I'm Pete, a tech blogger at @nobullshittech *(fictional)* from New York. I eliminate marketing bullshit from reviews of new technologies. (purpose)
2. **Second floor:** I test and analyze (analytical) new technologies and give them honest reviews (honesty) without excessive language (simplicity) because I want everyone to understand what these technologies can and cannot do.
3. **Third floor:** I publish a written review every Thursday and a video post every Saturday (diligence).
4. **Fourth floor:** So far, I've been working with XYZ. / My blog is supported by XZY (accuracy).

Fictional Pete just introduced himself in exactly 60 seconds, using four 15 second message stacks to stay within the short attention span theory. Between the ground and the first floor, the initial 15 seconds, he gave his conversation partner everything he needed to look him up after the conversation. Afterwards, he added more information as he got more time between floors. Pete was modest in the way he sold himself, but convincing. With his straightforward but catchy introduction, he will definitely be remembered. What would you think about someone introducing himself like this to you? Would you look up his blog afterwards? I definitely would.

Brand message stacking has two powerful effects. Just imagine how powerful this is if you're a more introverted person and shy about talking to people you don't know. You can simply memorize and recite your message stack until you know it by heart. Having this memorized will boost your confidence to start a conversation because you have a surefire opener. Secondly, if you deliver an introduction that is professional, you will project a focused and composed vibe, and you will look like you know what you want. You'd be wise to remember that people who know what they want are generally the people we trust.

However, there's one more important thing to keep in mind: people generally like it when *you* listen while *they* are talking. Remember that while stacking your brand message. Try to speak for as little time as possible. Time yourself in advance to be sure that you can fit everything into 60 seconds. Give your conversation partner the chance to react to your pitch and ask you questions. That being said, here's the good news: You've finished the first part of your personal value proposition. The hardest part is done!

Define All Other Brand Messages

Personal brand messaging is not just about how you introduce yourself, it is also about the messages you send in general. Let's say you've successfully introduced yourself with your brand stack and the other person keeps up the conversation. What impression of you would you like that person to walk away with?

Brand messaging, in this context, means that you consistently demonstrate how you embody your values during that conversation. Let's take Fictional Pete once more. Brand messaging in his case means that he would demonstrate his analytical mindset in conversations and would provide accurate and honest responses. He would also continue to promote his brand purpose of helping people understand technologies better and would mention why this purpose is important to him. Outside of conversations, he would showcase this embodiment by getting involved in communities, events and discussions that align with his brand purpose and engage with them by sending messages that resemble his brand identity.

Acting on your values and your tone of voice is your brand messaging

All this about brand voice, messaging, identity and purpose sounds complicated, I know. But it's actually very simple if you are authentic. If you are authentic, then you don't have to think twice about how you present yourself. You must avoid making the mistake of adopting an unnatural communication style because you want to impress someone. It won't work, especially in the long run. Just be yourself, that's the best and most convincing resource you have at your disposal! How do you feel about your messaging now? Do you have a clear idea of how you want to present yourself? Did the elevator exercise work for you? If yes, let's continue to the next chapter and start defining your skills!

Step 4: Matching Your Skills

You may be wondering why we are talking about skills this late in the process instead of right at the beginning. There's a simple reason for that– because it is secondary. Former Porsche CEO Peter Schutz once said: "Hire for character, train for skill." Investor and business tycoon Warren Buffett went further by saying: "In looking for people to hire, you look for three qualities: integrity, intelligence, and energy. And if they don't have the first, the other two will kill you." It is easier to train a person with good character to do a great job than to develop character in a skilled, but unscrupulous person. This principle does not apply only to hiring people, it is also the case for investors, networking situations and selling products. That is why it's more important to understand yourself and which personality traits you have to offer, before learning how to talk about your skills.

Why do some people get promoted even when better candidates are available? Why do some people get all the investor deals even though they don't yet have a product to show? The answer is because these people know how to sell themselves. Often your success rate depends on how you sell **yourself**, not your skills. What matters here is if people buy into what you're selling and trust **you** to be the right person with the right attitude to solve their problems. Having the skills is a presupposed requirement. It's extremely important to internalize this fact.

> *People buy, promote, connect and invest in you first,*
> *and in your skills second.*

That's why we've spent all this time defining the first part of your brand.

The Imposter Monster

This section is especially for people who suffer from imposter syndrome.

I almost always see my clients struggle to define what they're actually good at. Deep down you're probably aware of your skills, but perhaps saying what they are out loud makes you uncomfortable? Would you feel like you're showing off? Are you even allowed to complement yourself? If any of these describe you, don't worry. You're not alone. We live in a society in which being proud of our skills, even when it's justified, is discouraged. But there's nothing wrong with knowing what you bring to the table and vocalizing that. It's just important that you stay honest and authentic. But we'll talk more about that in the next chapter.

Previously, we looked inwards to investigate what you stand for and what your values are. In the following chapters, we'll look outwards and determine what you bring to the table and what your current status quo is. We'll ask questions like: What are my skills? What am I good at? What am I striving for? What skills make me unique? What skills do I have that are superior to others? Which of my skills do people value the most – at work and in my private life? Are you ready? Then let's get started.

You And Your Unique Skill Set

Do you remember the GROW goal framework from the goal setting chapter? We first looked at the **G**oal and then at the current **R**eality. Now, I'd like you to use the framework to check the progress of your brand building process. This is a good time to gauge if the brand you've created so far matches your reality.

What do you want your brand to stand for? Are you living by those values every day? What are you doing at the moment to align your actions with those values?

PRACTICE QUESTIONS

You should ask the same questions about your skills.

Which skills do you want people to associate with your brand? What expertise would you like to advertise?

Now, let's take a look at reality. What does it take to be an expert in your desired topic? Are you already an expert on this topic?

I know these aren't easy questions, and that they can be very scary to answer. But the truth is that we are all afraid that, at some point, people will find out that we're not as good as we say we are and we all dread the moment that we become exposed as phonies, frauds and liars.

I'm aware that this sounds harsh and that there's probably a little voice inside your head saying: How could she? Who does she think she is? Didn't she just say that I should believe in myself and overcome the imposter syndrome?

But let's face it, when you build a personal brand, you have a responsibility. The responsibility to live up to your image. To deliver what you promise or to overdeliver on your promise. Building a brand is hard work. You invest too much to build it on lies. You can compare your personal brand with a business. If Coca Cola advertises Sprite as a sweet, carbonated refresher, then you expect to get exactly that when you purchase a bottle. Imagine, you open one bottle after another and none of the Sprites are carbonated. Would you ever buy this product again? Would you trust Coca Cola? Probably not. If you promise something, you need to deliver on it. Both as a company and as an individual.

This has nothing to do with not being good at something. Just choose the things you're good at and focus on them.

Underpromise and Overdeliver

I'm not saying that you should stagnate and only focus on what you're already good at without evolving your skills. To the contrary, you absolutely should keep learning and improving your skills.

I mention this because it is often at this point that clients ask me: "How can I tell people that I'm a visionary, that I keep learning and that I evolve without compromising my expertise?" These are valid questions! Obviously, skills aren't static. Skills change and evolve, and with that the range of what your brand can offer expands.

Just be honest with yourself about what you can deliver right now. Don't sell yourself as a software engineer if you have never written a line of code. Everything looks good on paper until the moment you need to deliver.

To put this into perspective, I will tell you a little story about myself.

While studying for my master's degree, I focused on how criminals communicate online. Given my background in communications, I focused primarily on the communication part and paid only a little attention to the technical aspects. However, over time I felt that I needed to be capable of some coding basics to make a name for myself in the field. So, I started taking HTML and Python courses on codecademy.com. About one-third into the two courses, I gave up because I was simply not made to be a programmer. My strengths lie elsewhere (surprise!). But what did I do despite knowing that? I put HTML and Python on my CV and applied for jobs as a Cyber Security Analyst. Hilarious, isn't it? When no one replied to my applications, I was devastated. Again, hilarious, right? Today I know why. My personal brand was unfocused and completely inauthentic. I wanted to be everything to everyone and promised everything to everyone just to attract anyone. In the end, I didn't attract a single person. The only thing I got was likely a couple of laughs from the HR representatives at those companies.

The main takeaway from my experience is: Just be honest. Keep learning, keep evolving, but only claim the skills you truly have, meaning the ones you can provide within short notice. Only adapt your offering when your skillset has actually changed. Promoting skills in any other way will hurt your brand and might destroy people's trust in you. If people get more than you promised and more than they expected, they will refer to you as an expert.

> *Don't sell yourself short, but underpromise and overdeliver!*

That being said, remember that no one can be an expert and confident in everything. That's a fundamental and universal truth. More often than not, successful people become successful because they excel in one particular topic. It's their area of expertise and it's that area they've focused all their attention on. That's why they're so good at it. Do you think it's a problem for them that they can't brand themselves for other areas and even have to admit that they're less knowledgeable in them? Quite the opposite actually.

Let's look at a really simple example to visualise this. Let's take your favourite pizza restaurant. The pizza maestro has perfected his pizza dough, tomato sauce and oven temperature over many years until he came up with that incredible pizza you enjoy eating so much. He can be very confident about the product he's offering, simply because he's an expert in it. Now, let's say, he suddenly adds Thai food to his menu. What would your reaction be? Can he be an expert for pizza and Thai curry at the same time?

Haa… there we go. It doesn't feel right, does it? Not being an expert in other domains and branding himself for nothing but pizza actually makes him more credible, and with that, more successful.

PRACTICE EXERCISES

That being said, let's do a few exercises to identify the skills that help you promote an authentic personal brand, elevate your expert status and get you to your goal.

1. How have you presented yourself until now?

    Think back to situations in which you introduced yourself to a stranger. How did you do it? What did you introduce yourself as? Which of your skills did you promote? What is written on your LinkedIn profile? What about your CV? How did people react when you introduced yourself? What skills have you received positive feedback on?

    Write down at least 10 skills and rate them from 0-3 with three being very skilled and zero being not proficient. Be brutally honest in your assessment. If you're good, admit it. If you're not, own up to it and accept it.

2. What can you confidently deliver?

    Imagine, someone contacts you tomorrow asking you to deliver on all of the things your brand promises (to make this easier, think about what appears on your LinkedIn profile, or what you wrote on your CV or on your About page).

a. Which of those things can you confidently deliver today?

b. Which of those things do you need to spend a few days freshening up on before you can deliver them?

c. Which promises did you make because they sound good, but aren't actually something you can confidently deliver?

If you're having a hard time answering these questions and you're filled with self-doubt about your skills, don't get discouraged. That's just the imposter syndrome saying 'Hi'! Ignore it. You have noteworthy skills, I promise you. Keep reading. In the next exercises you'll identify them, in case you haven't already. Let's take a closer look so that we can continue building your highly-effective personal brand!

Everyone Has Skills Worth Promoting

Hello, imposter syndrome. It's good that you're showing up now, so that we can get rid of you once and for all. There's no room for self doubt in personal branding.

Everyone has skills. Everyone is good at something because everyone is unique. Your uniqueness alone is special. Some people are skilled in conventional ways, like being good at math, being a brilliant musician or successful at business. Others are skilled in more subtle ways, such as having great insights into human nature, being empathetic or having the ability to easily connect with people.

All of these are skills, and we all have them in some way or another, including you! Don't be discouraged!

Remember, successful people are successful, because they're authentic. Whatever is authentic to you can make you successful. Don't alter your personality or skill set to be something that's fake. Whatever is authentic and unique to you, is your best bet! I promise.

Focus on Your Skills, Not Someone Else's

The main message I want you to take away from this chapter is that you need to believe in yourself. You have unique skills. Everyone does. And those skills are worth promoting. But skills that are inauthentic to you and were simply acquired to impress others aren't worth promoting. Take the time to find out what you want, what skills you are proud of and ignore everyone and everything around you. Once you've done that, focus on those skills. Shape them, practice them, advance them. This is how you secure sustained uniqueness and success!

PRACTICE EXERCISE

Let's return to the exercise we did in the previous chapter. How many skills did you label with a three? Given what you've just learned, go back and assess them again. Are these the skills you want to promote? Are these skills taking you exactly where **you** want to go?

If so, say them out loud. Create a sentence like the following for each of those skills: "My name is Pete and I'm a great writer."

How does it make you feel to say these affirmations out loud? Does it make you proud?

To be honest, I initially thought that this exercise was weird and, for a long time, I didn't understand its power. That is, until I actually did it. My opinion changed because I realized that when you do this exercise, you begin to psychologically identify yourself with those skills the more often you say these sentences out loud. Remember the previous section about the importance of personally identifying with your goal and habits? This is it. This is how you can strengthen your association with your skills to focus on productive habits and get you to your goal.

Just think about it. Whenever you say "I am a writer" it does something to you, right? There's no going back after this. But remember to associate yourself with skills that you have. Telling myself that I'm a programmer won't do the trick. Stay honest and authentic, and this exercise will do magic - I promise!

Promote Skills That Get You to Your Goal

Stoicism, the ancient Greek school of philosophy, presents the idea that individuals should define their life goal and focus only on the things that get them there. Everything else is irrelevant. This approach is also the golden rule for maintaining a successful personal brand.

Think about it for a second. If your values, skills and message align and you only do things that align with them, people will know exactly what they're going to get from you. There's no confusion and no surprises. You can apply the same principle to achieving your brand goals. If you focus exclusively on developing the skills that are unique, authentic to you, you're walking straight up the ladder instead of falling off at every step.

Makes sense, right?

To summarize these points, I'd like you to complete a short exercise.

PRACTISE QUESTIONS

1. Think about your goal. How does it match your authentic skills? If they do not match, what do you need to adapt? Your goal or your skills?

2. Take out the value list you previously worked on. How do your values align with your skills? Do they emphasize your skills?

3. Look at your brand identity. Do your skills enhance the brand image (purpose, voice and messaging) you've built so far?

I think by now it's pretty clear that you must focus on **your** authentic skills in order for your personal brand to be successful. Don't waste time with skills you think others expect you to have or skills you think others will like. Now, we can add another sentence to your value proposition. A sentence about your skills. Choose the top one or two skills that are most relevant to your brand image. But before we get started, let's take a look at how our tech blogger Fictional Pete would do this. So far, his value proposition read as follows:

> *I'm Pete, a tech blogger at @nobullshittech (*fictional). I eliminate marketing bullshit from reviews about new technologies. I test and analyze new technologies and give them honest reviews without excessive language because I want everyone to understand what these technologies can and cannot do.*

Now, let's add his skills to the value proposition. Pete wants to promote himself as a writer and the authentic skills that align with his values and purpose are the ability to be precise and explain complex ideas simply. How can we express this in one sentence?

Here's one option: "I stand for simplicity, which is embodied in each of my short and concise tech reviews."

Since "I'm a tech blogger" appears at the beginning, Pete doesn't need to write "I'm a writer" again. Depending on the sophistication of the target group, he could change the sentence to "I'm a tech writer". However, calling Pete a blogger sounds more relatable, which is exactly the type of relationship he wants to establish with his readers. Next, we must include his skill to cut through the noise, extract relevant information and summarize it concisely. Being precise, simple and short in his writing is something his audience will appreciate because they are coming to him for analytical and concise articles to quickly get the information they need. Hence, mentioning this skill is an effective strategy to show his audience how his personal brand solves their problems. Importantly, when Pete sells himself to his audience like this, he is making a promise about what he will deliver. If he lives up to his promise, people will refer to him as the blogger with the concise tech reviews. They'll recommend him to others and spread the word about his blog. That is the power of successful personal branding!

Brand Promises and Responsibilities

Your value proposition is a promise to your audience and with that comes responsibility, as is the case with every brand. The more authentic your brand is, the less stressful upholding this responsibility will be.

Take Pete. His top skill is simplifying complex topics. For Pete, this is easy to do. It is something he does naturally all the time. So, it's actually very little effort for him to deliver his brand promise of regularly producing concise tech reviews. For someone like me who's not skilled at simplifying technology, delivering on this promise would be incredibly difficult, if not impossible. But that's because I have other skills, so I focus on what comes naturally to me and is aligned with my personal brand. If you want to create a successful personal brand, you must do the same.

So, what skills do you want to highlight in your value proposition? Which skills will get you where you want to go? Which are authentic to you and your goals? Write them down, form a sentence and add it to your value proposition. Once you're done, continue to the next section.

Step 5: Exploring Your Added Value

You've come such a long way and we've covered so much, which is why I'd like to have a quick recap here before we continue: So far, you've set your goals, defined your values, shaped your brand image with a brand purpose, identified your brand tone of voice and messaging and you matched your skills with your brand. Phew...that's quite a lot! Pat yourself on the back. Digging deep and defining these elements of your brand is hard work.

That you have made it so far speaks volumes for your dedication. And, as you know by now, consistency and dedication are crucial to building a powerful personal brand. The fact that you've been dedicated enough to work through this book suggests that a bright future awaits your brand. In fact, you've finished more than half of the steps included in the Ladder to Uniqueness. Four steps down, two more to go until you have your final value proposition. Are you excited? Then let's get started!

Discover What Makes You Stand Out

In this chapter, we're going to look at what your added value is or, in other words, the skills you have that differentiate you from others. This is what you will tell people they can only get from you.

You've probably noticed that I keep repeating the importance of authenticity. Trust me, there's a reason for that. As you climb the Ladder to Uniqueness and refine your personal brand while doing so, operating on inauthentic values only gets harder. Authenticity is your oxygen tank. When at the bottom of the ladder, you can still get by without an oxygen tank, but the higher you get, the harder it is to continue climbing without one. This chapter is the oxygen tank or authenticity benchmark. Why? Because now we will uncover what only you have to offer. It doesn't get any more personal and authentic than this. Comparing yourself to others and what they are doing won't work anymore. Identifying what makes you unique is an important step because this is where you discover what sets you apart from others. What makes your audience choose you instead of someone else. This is what differentiates you and makes your brand stand out and gain special recognition.

As we've discussed, the problem with branding is that most people look outwards and copy what other successful people are doing. That's where their own brand building stops as a result of skipping the added value step. But, the good news for you is that if you take this step seriously, you'll end up ahead. You will be the one who stands out because you went that extra mile to define an authentic brand and your added value. Ready? Then let's give it a try. Don't be discouraged if you find this step difficult. I'm right here by your side.

Find Your Unique Brand Angle

Our main task here is to discover what makes you unique and how you can use this to your brand's advantage in the market. We can achieve this with a relatively simple exercise.

PRACTICE EXERCISE

Look at your current value proposition. Let's take a good look at the values, purpose and skills you've written down over the course of working through this book.

What do you see? Is there a unified picture? As in, do you feel your goal, values, brand image and identity and skills align? Are they promoting your most authentic self?

> *In order to be irreplaceable, one must always be different.* - Coco Chanel

If you do see a unified picture, go online and start researching the people who offer similar services so that you can begin distinguishing your brand. Your research might include looking at the accounts of other job candidates, other startups, other writers, other influencers, or other blogs. You must tailor your research to your goal, and it can therefore include almost anything. As long as you're looking at people, businesses or services that exist in the same sphere as your brand.

Next, look at their messaging, the way they present themselves, what they offer, the values they promote and their communication style. Summarize all of this information on a sheet of paper (in soft or hard copy). You can download a free template from my website that will help you keep track of your findings. Next, compare your findings with your own offering and find the points where you differ and where you're similar. You can work with a simple +, - and 0 to help you visualize this. A + signifies that your offer is better or different, while a - means you're offering is less, and 0 indicates that your offers are equal. Do this with all of your research findings. Once you've done this, highlight all the pluses and then copy these items onto a separate document (I have a free template for this as well, if you like). Now, you should have a comprehensive list of all the aspects that make you different and better than your competitors. Summarize your findings in one sentence and include them in your value proposition.

If everything has made sense until now, awesome! If not, the example below will make it easier for you to get started.

Pete to the Rescue

Let's talk about Fictional Pete, our tech blogger from New York, again. His current value proposition is:

> *I'm a tech blogger for @nobullshittech (*fictional). I test and analyze new technologies and write honest reviews, cutting out all flowery verbiage so that everyone can understand what technologies can and cannot do. I stand for simplicity, which is embodied in each one of my short and concise tech reviews.*

To find Pete's added value, he goes online and researches his competitors' values, their messaging, their purpose and their unique offerings. For every competitor he asks, what can I do that they do not offer? And the other way around. He collects all this info and compares. The goal here is not to adapt his personal brand to a niche, he may or may not find, but to find opportunities that are already there and which he can utilize with his unique personal brand.

Pete's concise writing style makes him unique. He also notices that he's one of the few bloggers who is committed to eliminating the marketing speech around new technologies and explaining what technologies can and cannot do in simple terms. But what really sets Pete apart is the combination of simplicity and sarcasm that appears in his reviews. This is his added value. These are the things that make his personal brand recognizable.

How can he apply this to his value proposition? A value proposition is a work in progress until you have completed the last step on the Ladder to Uniqueness. With every step you take, adapt and rewrite your value proposition based on your new insights. Don't forget that your value proposition should be sharp and consist of as few sentences as possible, so follow Pete's lead and be concise. Everything related to your personal brand should be crisp and catchy. So, after completing this exercise, Pete's value proposition looks like this:

I'm Pete, a tech blogger and the founder of @nobullshittech. I write simple reviews about complicated technologies. By eliminating all marketing verbiage, I explain what technologies can and cannot do in an analytical and concise fashion, with a twist of sarcasm.

What do you think? Does Pete's value proposition represent his values, brand identity and added value well? Will this value proposition help him make a name for himself as a blogger? If you haven't completed this exercise yet, now is the right time. Afterwards, share the current state of your value propositions and let me know how it went! As soon as you're ready to go, let's continue to the next section where you'll define your market fit.

Step 6: Discovering Your Market Fit

You've climbed to the last step of the Ladder to Uniqueness! Great job! You're done asking deep (and often painful) questions. In this chapter, you will conclude your value proposition by finding your personal opportunity sweet spot.

Are you wondering why we are doing this so late in the game? Don't worry, there's a good reason for why I placed this step at the end. There's one common mistake that people often make when building their personal brands. First, they research the market's demands and then they accommodate their personal brand to that window of opportunity. By now you should scream out loud when you hear that. By now all your alarm bells should start ringing and you should be shouting: REMAIN AUTHENTIC!

Let's go back to Fictional Pete again. He could have browsed through Twitter and searched for popular blogs, copied his findings and built a brand for a target group based on that. The challenge with this approach is that he might not be skilled enough to serve this target group and it could take him a while to be on par with the popular, established blogs that already made a name for themselves and occupy that particular group and market share. He might be mildly successful, but it's risky and a lot of work if he wants to make it in a market that's already occupied by others. What he should do instead is find an opportunity niche where his unique skill set and personality attract people who are receptive to exactly that offering. To get there, he first needs to define what he wants to do and what he can deliver with full confidence and then go out, browse Twitter to find the target group(s) in need of what he has to offer and test his idea with them. The smaller the niche, the higher the chance to get a kick-start. This is why the market step is at the very end of the Ladder to Uniqueness. Don't forget, you need to know what you stand for to stand out. You need to have a stable foundation to reach your biggest goals!

The Personal Brand Funnel

Now that your foundation is built, you can find the right market fit for your brand promise. We're not browsing the market to adapt your brand (which is what most people do). What I'm going to help you do now is find the right market for your established personal brand.

From now on, your only job is to find the kind of people who will be most receptive to your brand image and promise. This is how you'll have the highest chances of success.

Allow me to compare this with the funnel logic that is applied in sales and marketing. The goal of a funnel logic is to take the guessing out of the sales process and predict success rates by qualifying customers. Qualifying a customer basically means that you label him with a 'plus' or 'minus' depending on how likely he is to engage, interact or buy from you. This labelling or qualifying happens every time a customer interacts with the brand. Similar to pouring liquid down a funnel, which is wide at the top and narrow at the bottom, the goal of sales and marketing in this context is to narrow the audience size down to the people with the most amount of 'pluses', meaning people who are very engaged and therefore very likely to make purchases. If a customer is in the narrow area of your funnel, meaning he's a highly qualified lead, there's almost a 100% guarantee that he'll become a customer/reader/follower. These people are golden opportunities and require special care and focus, because they're your 'hottest' leads.

We'll use a similar approach to discover your market fit in the next section. The goal is to find that narrow, highly qualified opportunity spot where there's nearly a 100% guarantee that they'll be receptive of your personal brand and offering. Concretely, we'll narrow a huge pool of potential target groups down to a selection that is likely to respond positively to your brand image and promise. This way, you're not leaving anything to chance.

Ready? Then let's get cracking!

Find Your Opportunity Spot in the Market

This is the last part of the Ladder to Uniqueness, you're almost done! Now, we'll apply the funnel logic to narrow that target group down to a portion that is most likely to positively interact with your brand. Afterwards, your value proposition will be complete. Remember, the objective here is to find an opportunity sweet spot within the market for your unique brand.

Define Your Target Group

If you look at Pete's value proposition from the previous chapter:

I'm Pete, a tech blogger and the founder of @nobullshittech. I write simple reviews about complicated technologies. By eliminating all marketing verbiage, I explain what technologies can and cannot do in an analytical and concise fashion, with a twist of sarcasm.

What kind of people would respond to his brand promise? Can this be classified as one target group or more? Are those target groups very different or similar? How old are they? Where do they hang out? What are they interested in?

The people who are most likely to respond to Pete's brand promise are likely those who buy the 'XYZ for dummies' books. Basically, this group seeks services that describe complex topics in a simple manner. These people likely work in non-tech positions but are interested in new trends and developments. Collectively, these people fall into one target group. But another target group would also likely respond to Pete's brand promise. Tech fans who appreciate analytical reviews and despise excessive marketing speech. People who'll appreciate his reviews for their precision, accuracy and dedication to technology.

There are two completely different target groups and yet, Pete can address both of their needs with one value proposition. The value proposition we previously outlined works for both, because he didn't look at the market first and built a value proposition for that, but looked inward first and built a value proposition for his personality and skills. And that is adaptable to multiple target groups. This is the magic of adapting the market to fit your brand and not the other way around. But now enough about Pete. Let's get started with finding your market fit.

PRACTICE EXERCISE

Refer to your competitor evaluation sheet from the previous chapter and add a column called market fit. Just like Pete did, do some research to figure out which audiences your competitors are targeting.

How can you find out which target groups your competitors are talking to? The easiest way is to go on their social media profiles. Once you're there, you have a couple of options:

1. **Browse the "About" and profile descriptions:** Most people describe the target audience they hope to attract in their profile descriptions or on their "About" pages. Write those target groups down.

2. **Browse their follower lists:** Check out the profiles of those followers and make notes about the things they are writing about, like their background, their education etc., whatever attributes you deem important.

3. **Browse their hashtags:** Check their hashtags and general tags. What kind of audiences are they targeting with those? Research what kind of people follow those hashtags.

4. **Browse their comments:** Find out what kind of people leave comments. Go to their profiles and find out everything you can about their preferences, activities and so on.

5. **Browse their blog:** Check what audiences your competitors target with the topics they write about on their blog. If you can identify themes, search for them on social media, online forums and so on. You should also find out what kind of audience responds to such topics.

Document this information in one place, if possible, on the worksheet. You're now at the very top of the funnel. The wide opening of the cone. In the next step, we'll start narrowing your target audience down in order to find the perfect market fit for your personal brand.

Narrow Down Your Personal Brand Funnel

By now you should have added all your research findings onto the worksheet. Keep that sheet handy. In the previous skills exercise, you used the +, - and 0 method to assess how you compare to your competitors. Of these, you highlighted the ones that you have a competitive advantage over, meaning that what you and your brand have to offer is either better or different. Going forward, delete all competitors but the highlighted ones. (But don't forget to make a copy of the worksheet before deleting it. You don't want to lose all the research data you collected on the other competitors). By doing so, you significantly reduce your prospective target audiences and move one step downwards in your funnel.

How? Since you already know that you have more or something different to offer than the highlighted competitors, it should be relatively easy to persuade their target audiences to be interested in you. And with that, you have your first prospective target group(s). However, we still haven't discovered your market fit. Now, your job is to find the people in those target groups who will be receptive to a better brand, to a better offer and, essentially, a better experience. Meaning, find the ones who aren't diehard fans or are very engaged with your competitor. Find the ones who are more neutral and easier to persuade. In order to do that, go through your notes or repeat the exercise from above in depth. You're looking for details now, not a general overview.

Let's see how Pete went about it. During his research, he found out that most tech review blogs target males between 18-50 years of age. Most of them are gadget fans with a vast knowledge of technology. Targeting the exact same target group would make it difficult for Pete to succeed, right? The competition is too high for the beginning, because it is huge and populated by other blogs. That's why Pete proceeds by only looking at the cases in which his services are superior. He is precise and objective. Pete then searches his competitors' followers for people working in statistics, physics and biology because they might appreciate tech reviews that focus purely on technology. He also focuses on lawyers and bureaucrats, people who aren't too familiar with technology and might appreciate how concise and simple his reviews are. Now, go through your findings on the worksheet and try to find niche target groups just like in Pete's example. And that's how you define your unique opportunity sweet spot and find the target groups with which you have the highest chances of success.

And this is the end of the Ladder to Uniqueness. You did it! You climbed all the way up. If you're unsure about any of the steps and would like some guidance, then it's time to book a session and get clarity. From here, we'll look at your value proposition once more and I'll provide you with a few tips and tricks for how to successfully apply your personal brand!

Conclusion

It's incredible how far you've come. There's only one small step left now. You should be pretty confident about the value proposition you've created. At this point, your value proposition should convey who you are, what you value, and it should include your skills and the unique aspects of your personality. After all, your value proposition should appeal to a target group that will get you to the goal you defined at the very beginning.

In case you want to go through each step once more, here's a short recap:

Set Your Goal

What do you want to achieve and how can your personal brand get you there? Remember that achievable goals are SMART, PURE and CLEAR and the best way to define them is to use the GROW goal setting framework.

Pete's example:

> **Grow**: I want to increase my mailing list by 3K subscribers within the next 6 months (timebound, measurable, specific, realistic & achievable).

> **Reality**: As of today, I have acquired 5K subscribers within 12 months by posting on Twitter, Reddit and other platforms. I've done guest posts and appeared in a few podcasts to increase awareness.

> **Options**: I could do advertising, buy ads in newsletters etc.; I could create a consistent brand image for my blog to present it as the place to go for no-bullshit tech reviews. This will help me generate publicity and get recognized

> **Will**: I work fulltime on this blog and am willing to put in extra hours to achieve my goal. I'm also willing to invest $1.000 to achieve this goal within 6 months.

Define Your Values

Remember, values are principles or standards of behavior and one's judgement of what is important in life. What are your principles? Who are you and what do you stand for? Which values do you want to be associated with? To help you answer these questions, check out this extensive list of values and choose 10 that best define you.

Pete's example:

> Sensitivity, fairness, accuracy, service, simplicity, diligence, analytical and honesty.

Shaping Your Image

Define your brand purpose, a purpose that establishes an emotional connection with your audience and motivates you to work for more reasons than just to make money. Then, determine the tone of voice and message that fit with your values, goal and purpose. Remember to use the brand message stacking method.

Pete's example:

> Pete's purpose is to help people buy technology they understand instead of falling for marketing traps. His voice and messaging is simple, analytical, moderately sarcastic and concise.

Matching Your Skills

What do you bring to the table? What are the skills others value you for? Which skills are solid and which are in development or non-existent?

Pete's example:

> Pete is an engineer and a talented writer. Thanks to his skill set, he has the ability to see technologies for what they are and describe them in simple language.

Exploring Your Added Value

What are you doing better than others? What are you doing different than others? Compare your brand purpose, tone of voice, messaging and skills with your competitors to find out what sets you apart.

Pete's example:

> Pete's added value is the ability to deconstruct complex topics and explain them in simple language. He pairs his analytical and precise writing with sarcasm and makes tech reviews fun to read.

Discovering Your Market Fit

Don't make your personal brand fit wherever there is demand in the market, you should rather find a niche in the market that fits your personal brand. Who will be most receptive to your message? Who among your competitor's audience will be easy to swing?

Pete's example:

> Pete's most qualified target groups are the 'for dummy' readers and scientists. These people want content that explains complex technologies in simple language and/or they appreciate concise, non-marketing, straight-to-the-point articles. With this awareness, Pete knows to target physicists, biologists and bureaucrats, for example.

After all these steps, his final value proposition sounds like this:

I'm Pete, a tech blogger and the founder of @nobullshittech. I write simple reviews about complicated technologies. By eliminating all marketing verbiage, I explain what technologies can and cannot do in an analytical and concise fashion, with a twist of sarcasm.

And what about yours? What does your value proposition look like? If you'd like to share it with me via LinkedIn, Twitter or email, I'd be happy to give you feedback on it. This is the end of the Ladder to Uniqueness. If you're not yet convinced by your value proposition and brand image, reach out to me. We will nail this together!

SECTION 3

Use Your Highly Effective Personal Brand

5 Situations Where Personal Branding Makes You More Successful

Wow, the time has come. You're ready to put yourself out there. How confident are you about doing this? How do you feel about presenting yourself alongside your brand image from now on?

Based on my experience working with clients, this is usually a big moment. Many of my clients have been both nervous and excited upon concluding their journeys. They were proud of owning a highly effective brand, but nervous about what it meant to have one. If you are experiencing similar feelings, I can calm you down. A personal brand is there to enable you. It is there to give you confidence, to make it easier to connect with people and to get you ahead. Be proud of what you've achieved and of the fact that you're one of the very few people who now owns a personal brand.

Keeping that in mind, I suggest you take the first step to inform people about your personal brand. Go public with it. Now! Send a tweet asking your target group for feedback. A simple "Hey, I've been working on a personal value proposition recently. What do you think?" will do. Feel free to tag me in this post if that gives you more confidence. Ask your friends, colleagues and family if they think your personal brand aligns with who you are. Publish your value proposition on your career profiles, "About" pages and in your profile descriptions. Basically, wherever you are you should introduce yourself with your value proposition. This is how you will get used to it quickly.

People's reactions will motivate you, I promise!

Apply Your Personal Brand

Since your personal brand's brand identity is also part of your personal identity, you carry your brand with you at all times. However, there are special situations in which promoting your personal brand will make a huge difference. It will get you ahead and differentiate you from your competitors. Those are the situations in which your brand shows that you are the best, most unique and special solution to their problem! That's why we're here thinking about personal branding after all, right?

There is an unlimited number of such situations, but I will elaborate on a few key ones, like job interviews, networking events, work promotions, and working with investors and online communities. However, I'm interested in knowing which situations you've utilized your brand in and experienced a positive outcome. Feel free to tweet your experiences and stories to me.

Job Interviews

How can you use your personal brand in job interviews? Companies hiring today have a massive pool of talented candidates to pick from. They will choose the best cherries they can find. To win that competition, you have to be the best cherry and here's how you can do that.

> Be honest

One of the biggest mistakes is trying to be everything to everyone (I did this a million times before realizing that it's a waste of time!), especially when we feel pressured to find a job. We try to tailor our CV to every job posting that is remotely related and modify stories in our cover letters.

The thing is: no one is an expert in everything, and even if a company buys into this, the moment they test you on it they'll see your true potential. So, save everyone some time and be honest!

If you want to stand out, you have to be a convincing expert. Experts are extremely knowledgeable in one and excel in that. Experts are cherries. Focus on one thing that you do well and highlight that. Make your personal brand all about this skill.

> Be brave

What I'll say next is scary. I know, because I've personally been there and because my clients get scared every time.

Reduce the number of companies you apply to. Look at your value statement and brainstorm the kind of companies that could appeal to a person like you: a person with your skills, values and motivations.

Remember the funnel logic that helps you narrow down a big audience into a smaller, more applicable group? You can apply that here as well. You want to find the few companies that align so well with who you are, what you're capable of and what they're looking for, that there's very little chance they won't be interested in you.

I know that the idea is scary because it requires you to spend a lot of time sifting through companies and preparing targeted applications. In the meantime, it's true that you could have sent out applications to a lot more companies instead. But remember, there are few openings and a lot of applicants, most of whom will take the latter application approach.

Imagine you're in HR choosing the applicants you want to interview. If out of 50 applications, one person made an effort to think how their skill set matches the position, you'd choose them, right? That one person could be you.

> **Be smart**

Now it's time to prepare your application. A cover letter and CV alone won't do, that's clear. If you want to stand out, you have to do more. You have to evidence that what your brand and value proposition promise is true.

You have to give the company a quick glimpse of what you can do for them, instead of making it difficult for them to find it by reading your letter and resume.

How can you do that? Present what you preach. If you are selling yourself as a marketing strategist, apply with a marketing strategy. Show them what kind of strategy you would propose if you were hired. If you are selling yourself as a designer, send them designs they could use. If you apply as a software engineer, show them some code that they'll find interesting.

Don't just send a portfolio of things you've done in the past. Do something specific for them and focus on the particular skill you want to be seen as an expert for. Every aspect of your application should point to that skill. Make sure the company gets a convincing image of your expert status on this topic.

Or, let's say you are a generalist. With generalist I mean that you're not an expert in a specific domain, but rather an expert in coordinating domains on a high-level. In that case, you should promote high-level skills, such as coordinating multiple responsibilities and delegating them in an effective and efficient way.

> **Be prepared**

Prepare meticulously for every single interview. Leave nothing to chance. Always think: What is a person in this department, this position etc. interested in? What problem(s) can I solve for this person? And then prepare as many questions and answers as possible that you think this particular person might ask you. Your answers should consistently align with your brand and address your interviewer's business interests. Put your brand in every single answer.

You want everyone you engage with to have the same positive experience with your personal brand. You also want everyone to describe your brand with the same words. For example, if your value is creativity, each person, regardless of the department, should experience that you're creative. If you're collaborative, give each person an example of you being collaborative in a situation that matters to them. When you do this, you paint an image of who you are and what people will get from you. An image is always easier to grasp and comprehend. By creating a brand image, you make it easier for people to label you, which makes it easier for people to talk about you. And what you really want to achieve is grabbing people's attention. This will make it easier to talk and discuss your application. The longer you stay in people's minds, the higher the chances that you will get hired.

That's it. I've tried these techniques many times and they always work like a charm.

Getting a Promotion at Work

Positioning yourself as an expert in your area of work in your company is probably the single most important strategy needed to climb up the career ladder. Yes, you need to be skilled and smart, but if you don't know how to convey that, others will get that promotion or salary raise instead of you. Positioning and promoting a personal brand at the workplace helps you gain the trust of the people who matter – decision makers, colleagues, externals.

Think about your goal at your workplace. What do you want to achieve? Where do you want to go? Look at your value proposition and compare which of your features will help you get there. With which of your features, I mean which part(s) of your personal brand should you highlight how and to whom to achieve your desired goal? Don't change who you are, but promote what you already excel in. There's no place where it's harder and more detrimental to fake a personal brand than at your workplace. You spend so much time with your boss and colleagues every day that the people who matter eventually see who you really are. This is why you should never put a different personality forward. Stick to your brand! It makes you unique, it makes you look professional. And then remain consistent. Show your colleagues that they can rely on you and that they can trust you to deliver what you promise. Make it easy for people to trust, recommend and talk about you! This will make you the first and most preferred choice!

Networking

Owning your personal brand will make all the difference in every networking situation. No matter if you're networking internally in a company, externally at conferences and events, on social media or simply in your free time with people you don't know. The challenge with networking events is that people come there with a purpose and goal in mind. They want to meet people who are interesting to them and enrich their goal aspirations. Most people want to make connections that are a means to an end or said simpler: they want to tap into networks that might help them reach their goal more efficiently. That being said, you need to have two things in mind in order to be successful at a networking event.

> **Eye the competition**: You have a lot of competition and need to deal with short attention spans. If you've ever been to networking events, you might have noticed that people's eyes constantly wander while they're talking to you. People constantly screen the room for more interesting and 'useful'

people. If you want to prevent that and ensure that your conversation partner actually listens to you, you need to captivate them.

> **Be relevant**: In order to captivate someone in a sea of interesting people, you need to know who you're talking to, you need to understand what that person wants to get out of the event and then apply the brand message stacking method. Adapt the structure of your brand message (not the content, don't change who you are! Remain authentic!) and start with the first 15 second message that conveys the most relevant information about you that is also relevant to the person with whom you are speaking. Always keep in mind what that person is looking for and highlight the corresponding aspects of your personal brand.

Once you're done with your concise 60 second introduction, start asking questions. This part is particularly important at networking events. I will provide you with some critical insight: A human truth is that we all want to feel important. We want our lives to matter. We want to matter. There's nothing wrong with that. This aspiration continues to help us evolve. That inner motivation helps us strive to reach new levels and improve our status quo.

Why am I telling you this now? Because this fundamental human truth is particularly relevant to networking events. When we are surrounded by interesting people, we fear not being enough and looking boring or like losers. That's why you hear a lot of boasting and see a lot of egoism at these events. But you can use this to your advantage. Introduce yourself in 60 seconds, make it easy for others to grasp how you can help them and then give them the floor. Let them talk, ask insightful questions and add smart comments to the discussion. The more you listen, the more pleasantly you'll be perceived. And the more pleasant the experience, the more easily they'll remember you later on. That being said, always be empathetic with the person in front of you. Is it a person who values a good discussion? Then have a good discussion. If you're analytical, answer analytically. If you're creative, answer creatively or with creative examples. Remember your brand values and put yourself in the shoes of the other person to understand what he wants to get out of talking to you. Then, you are best equipped to give appropriate answers that are coated in your brand messaging and respond to your opponent's conversation goal.

The combination of an easy-to-remember brand message and a positive conversation experience is extremely powerful in networking. Make sure to follow up within 24 hours and remind your conversation partner(s) of the pleasant encounter. Since they will receive a lot of follow up messages, make it easy for him to remember you by introducing yourself with the same 15 seconds that you used to start your conversation. Then ask an insightful question, share an article or something that might be engaging enough for him to respond. Keep the entire follow up message to less than 5 sentences.

Investors

The challenges you face when networking are similar to the ones you experience when dealing with investors. When you seek the interest of investors, you compete for attention and trust with a large pool of qualified candidates. Your job? Stand out. Prove that you're the best investment they could make. Make them trust you. Personal branding is what sets entrepreneurs and startup founders apart. Let's quickly visualize how your personal brand will affect your success rate.

Typically, you gain attention through startup pitches, by attending networking events or having direct contact with investors. In these situations, it's vital to have a clear value proposition and a good elevator pitch (or brand stacking) in place so that you will grab everyone's attention. However, to attract an investor to work with you, you need to make them trust you. And that's where authenticity and consistency come into play! I've been repeating myself on this one because these two aspects make you fail or succeed. Investors receive innumerous pitches every day and what will set you apart is actually delivering what you promise in that pitch. That means be authentic and honest! It is the first step to gaining trust. The second step to gaining investors' trust is being consistent. They heard your pitch and value proposition and were hooked, now you need to show them that you're reliable. Deliver on your brand promise, brand message and skills every time you interact with them and in every action you take. That's how you show them that you're trustworthy and worthy of their investment.

Online Communities and Platforms

Regardless of whether you're an influencer or simply using online platforms to make yourself visible and heard, your key to success is creating a recognition factor for your profile and across your online platforms. This means you want to ensure that people recognize you immediately in their feed even without reading your name. And this should happen uniformly on all of the platforms you're using. Your personal brand will help you achieve exactly that. In the chapter 'Shaping your image', you determined your brand's promise, messaging and tone of voice. You also thought about the kind of imagery that would work best for your brand, the type of language and words a brand like yours would use and what type of stories and content your brand would generate.

When you're presenting your personal brand online, keep these elements in mind at all times. You want people to recognize you across all platforms based exclusively on how you present yourself in all the content (blogs, posts, articles, videos, etc.) you publish. You can check how you're doing on that front by searching your own name on Google. Do the results match with your brand image? Do they convey the same messages about who you are and how you want to be seen? If not, don't worry. You can start promoting your brand now and your search results will change over time. But continue to come back to those Google results and see how and if they change. If they are still inconsistent, reconsider if your communication is really in sync with your brand. Another important aspect of promoting yourself online is choosing platforms that work with your brand. On the one hand, think about which platforms align with your values, your skills and the brand promise you're promoting. Next, compare that with the platforms you currently use and find out whether your target audience also uses those platforms. If not, go back to Step Six and find out if you need to modify your target group(s) for your personal brand.

Before we conclude and hop over to the last chapter of the book, there's one last thing to say about building an online presence for your brand. It is inevitable that you will use some platforms primarily personal purposes and others for professional reasons. Always keep in mind that when people search for you they might also check out the personal accounts. To avoid any problems, make sure that the content on those pages doesn't contradict with the brand you promote and your position on other social media.

Tips and Tricks to Staying Consistent

We've talked about the different steps involved in creating a personal brand. You've completed multiple exercises, built your own brand and written your personal value statement. We also covered various scenarios in which your personal brand will elevate your chances of getting ahead, achieving success and standing out from the crowd. The only thing left to talk about now is how you can stick to your branding. I've talked a lot about being consistent, but I haven't told you how you can achieve that. But no worries, I've got you covered. In this chapter, we'll discuss two strategies that work very well for me and my clients. Once you've completed the next pages, you will have answers to questions like 'How can I remain consistent?' and 'What if I forget my messaging?'. Ready? Let's go.

Challenge Yourself

This is the moment where I emphasize authenticity again. The best strategy for not forgetting your messaging is to create an authentic brand based on values and skills that come naturally to you. That way, you don't have to rehearse a brand message, tone of voice and image. The image is who you already are.

That being said, even if you have an authentic brand and you're just beginning to promote and position yourself with your brand, you might have some anxiety and confusion about whether or not your actions align with the brand you've so carefully built. That's absolutely normal, so please don't worry about it. Like all good things, you need time and practice to start thinking from your brand's perspective. That's why the most powerful, and in my experience, the most successful method is to constantly question your actions. I don't mean questioning whether or not to do them, but how to do them. Whenever I engage with clients, publish posts and create content, I ask myself: How could I frame this better so that it is better aligned with my brand? Is there a better way? Does this appeal to my brand and my target group? If not, what does?

I challenge every word, activity, platform and idea with my brand in mind. Does this highlight who I am and what I have to offer? Or does it confuse and detract from my brand and messaging? More often than not, the answer to the latter question is 'YES'. It's frustrating and sometimes disappointing, but if you want to build a brand you need to be strict when making these decisions. In such cases, I just remind myself of the goal. The goal is to stand out, get recognition and be the first and preferred choice. If a great idea contradicts my goal or jeopardizes my standing, it's simply not a great idea, at least in that particular scenario. Be brave and brutally honest with yourself, it'll go a long way.

Form Habits

In addition to challenging every action's relevance to your value proposition, you can form habits that align with your personal brand and practice them until you internalize them and apply them automatically.

James Clear, author of the international bestseller 'Atomic Habits', developed an incredible method for creating long-term habits. Habits that stick. He calls this method habit stacking. Clear describes that we are most likely to stick to our habits if we modify them in small increments every single day. Over time, those habit changes accumulate and get us to exactly where we want to be so that we become who we want to be. In order to assure that your habits direct you towards your goals, he suggests connecting them, or 'stack[ing]' them.

You can apply this method to ensure that you remain consistent with your branding. I use this method and tell my clients to do the same. When explaining this to my clients, I advise them to create a schedule with very specific habits that improve internalizing their personal brand. Every task needs to be described as specifically as possible. The description must include the time that you are going to work on a task, what exactly needs to be done and a quick note on how it aligns with your brand. This process needs to be so clear and straightforward that it can be replicated every week.

But to make this clearer, let's refer again to Fictional Pete. Let's say Pete wants to make sure he'll be consistent with posting tech reviews that align with his brand. His habit stacking could appear as follows:

1. On Tuesday, after breakfast I will browse technologies for 60 min.

2. After that, I will choose one technology that fits my portfolio, aligns with my brand and looks potentially interesting for my target group.   Establishes a habit to pick a technology that aligns with his brand at an early stage before he begins writing the blog post.
3. On Wednesday after breakfast, I will request a demo or download the technology to play around with it for 90 minutes.   Establishes a habit to thoroughly understand the products that will be featured in his reviews.
4. While testing the technology, I'll make notes every time I discover something interesting or when I see that a product's marketing overpromised what it can do.   Establishes a habit to live up to his values of being analytical in pursuit of his brand promise to eliminate marketing verbiage.
5. On Wednesday after lunch, I will write the first draft for my review and brainstorm appealing headlines for my target group.
6. On Thursday after breakfast, I will spend 60 minutes editing the review to ensure that it contains simple language. I will also use this time to choose appropriate imagery and prepare my newsletter and outreach posts.   Establishes a habit to live up to his promise of explaining complex topics in simple language.
7. On Thursday after lunch, I will check if my brand messaging matches my review, posts and newsletter content. I will publish by 3pm at the latest.   Establishes a habit to promote a consistent brand image across all platforms.

And that's all there is to the magic. The easier you make it to execute those small steps, the easier it will be for you to internalize your new brand- and value-oriented habits. Once you've successfully adopted them, you'll choose topics and write or speak in ways that appeal to your audience without thinking twice. It is a very powerful method for elevating your personal brand.

Why? It's your path to being 100% authentic. If you create habits that align with your brand and follow through with them, everything you do will be in sync with your brand image. If you need further guidance developing a brand-oriented habit stack for yourself, you know where to find me. Feel free to schedule a call with me and we'll get it done together!

SECTION 4

Conclusion and Appendix

That being said, I can now announce that you're fully prepared to take your highly effective personal brand out into the world. You're equipped with everything you need to present a powerful image of yourself and achieve your goals.

I'm proud of you and you should be proud of yourself as well. This was a difficult process. Building a brand is hard work.

This is your competitive advantage; it is what will set you apart from others in the future! You walked that extra mile to understand who you are, what you have to offer and how you can reach the people who are receptive to your brand. You can now sell yourself with full confidence without being a show-off. You will be able to convince people and make them trust in your abilities and your potential. You will be the one who's getting those promotions, salary raises, deals, subscribers, followers and fans, not the others.

You are unique and now you know how to show your uniqueness to the world! Good luck! Don't forget to let me know how you liked the book in a review on Amazon.

For two free personal branding tips every Wednesday, subscribe to my mailing list: https://melaniegoel.com/

Referenced & Suggested Reading List

Branden, Nathaniel (1994). *The Six Pillars of Self-Esteem.* Bantam Books

Carnegie, Dale (1936, 1981, 2010). *How to Win Friends & Influence People.* Simon & Schuster

Clear, James (2018). *Atomic Habits.* Penguin Random House UK

Covey, Stephen R. (1989, 2004). *The 7 Habits of Highly Effective People.* Simon & Schuster

David, Susan (2016). *Emotional Agility.* Penguin Random House UKK

Duhigg, Charles (2012). *The Power of Habit.* Random House Books

Eyal, Nir & Li, Julie (2019). *Indistractable.* Bloomsbury

Goldsmith, Marshall (2015). *Triggers.* Crown Publishing Group

Hari, Johann (2018). *Lost Connections.* Bloomsbury

Holiday, Ryan (2016, 2017). *Ego Is the Enemy.* Penguin Random House LLC

Jeffers, Susan (1987, 2007, 2012). *Feel the Fear and Do it Anyway.* Penguin Random House UK

Neill, Michael (2009, 2018). *Supercoach: 10 Secrets to Transform Anyone's Life.* Hay House

Ries, Al & Trout, Jack (2001). *Positioning.* McGraw Hill

For more book tips, feel free to reach out to me directly via email.

www.ingramcontent.com/pod-product-compliance
Lightning Source LLC
Chambersburg PA
CBHW031432210526
45464CB00005B/2171